The Lover's Dance

REV. HELEN LEONA BROCK

The Lover's Dance
by Reverend Helen Leona Brock
Copyright ©2004 Reverend Helen Leona Brock

ISBN
For Worldwide Distribution
Printed in the U.S.A.

Second Printing 2012-2013

Table of Contents

PART I: TOTAL SURRENDER
Step 1: Worship...1
Step 2: Birth of Trust 11
Step 3: Learning to Hear His Voice 15
Step 4: Uprooting the "Little Foxes" 20
Step 5: Coming to the End of Self (Old Nature)...............34
Step 6: Final Sacrifice 39
Step 7: Final Sacrifice Completed Forever.......................44

PART II: NEW BEGINNING, NEW CREATION
Step 8: Resurrection Day 48
Step 9: Discovering His Gifts in Us 56

PART III: HIS ANOINTING
Step 10: Entering Into His Rest.......................................61

PART IV: THE FATHER'S ROYAL CHILDREN
Step 11: The Royal Overcomer 68
Step 12: The Royal Children Ruling and Reigning...........76

PART V: HIS TRANSFORMED BRIDE
Step 13: Outward Signs of Inward Transformation..........81
Step 14: Sons of God Revealed Through His
           New Creation Bride...85
Step 15: Exceptional Love..92

PART VI: THE BRIDEGROOM AND HIS BELOVED
Step 16: Within the Veil...95

PART VII: THE GLORY OF HIS PRESENCE
Step 17: Jesus—The Priceless Pearl...............................107
Step 18: Ribbons of Rejoicing 112

Dedication

I dedicate this book first and foremost to my gracious Heavenly Father who chose you and me to become the Bride of His precious and only begotten Son, Jesus. Secondly, to my Lord and Saviour Jesus, "Beautiful One," with whom I am passionately, madly and wildly in love and at whose feet I humbly bow. Thirdly, to Sweet Holy Spirit who taught me how to become an Intimate Worshipper through the beautiful Lover's Dance.

And to my wonderful husband, the late Dr. Joseph A. Brock, who showed me every day of our Christian marriage what it is like to be passionately loved by a man totally in love with his Lord and Saviour, our Lord Jesus Christ.

Acknowledgments

To my wonderful heavenly Father, to His precious Son, Jesus, and to the sweet Holy Spirit whom I adore with all my heart.

To my beautiful and loving family, which also now includes the blessing of my lovely goddaughter and her daughter here in Hawaii. You are all my precious children and together we have become His *ohana* (family). I love you all so very much.

A special *mahalo* (thank you) to precious Pastor and Mrs. Sapp and dear Mrs. Yasuhara and the late Pastor Yasuhara. For 20 years (1975-1995) your love and concern for all of us at First Assembly of God was (and still is) the foundation upon which we, your congregation, who are now all over Hawaii and the mainland, have built our lives. We love you so very much.

To my wonderful island-wide choir (early 1990s), I love you. To my former T.V. ministry programme partner, you are special. To my very special friend and daily prayer partner, I love you. To my gracious and young Christian hula *kumu* (teacher), He loves you so. To my First Assembly of God Ladies' Bible Study group (1993-95), you are precious.

To my many dearest brothers and sisters (natural and in the Lord), friends, neighbors, pastors, ministers, teachers, ministries both here in Hawaii and on the mainland, and everyone else who has ever played a part in my destiny, thank you. I would not be where I am today without your love, support, encouragement, and affirmation. May our Lord bless each and every one of you abundantly.

Foreword

The Lover's Dance, is very special for it is devoted to the most beautiful book of the Bible, *The Song of Solomon*. This wonderful little book in the Old Testament is the most passionate book in The Bible. It is through *The Song of Solomon* that you will come to understand just how deeply our Holy Lord longs for you, His Bride. He desires to have intimate time with His beautiful Bride; intimacy through His Holiness imparted to her as she begins to passionately fall in love with Him while sitting at His feet and worshipping.

If you have cried to Him from the depth of your heart and asked Him to teach you how to have this intimacy with Him, then He is answering your prayer through this precious book, *The Song of Solomon*, within *The Lover's Dance*. Oh sweet Bride! He loves you so! Come! Let's run together. "Let the king bring me into his chambers" (Song of Sol. 1:4b).

Step 1

Worship

Our Lord is so good. After my precious Christian physician husband of 27 years died in 1991, I was devastated. I adored him so. We did everything together, including worship of our precious Lord Jesus and daily prayer.

Just three months after his death and after having dried my tears for the millionth time, I said to the Lord, "Lord, I miss the passion and romance Joey and I had together more than anything else."

Suddenly, our Lord spoke to my heart and said, *"I'll be your Lover!"*

"How, Lord?" I asked out loud.

"Through *The Song of Solomon*," He said. "Every day just as you had intimate time together with your husband, you are now to have that same intimate time with Me. Just as you *never* allowed any distractions during your intimate time together, *do not allow any distractions during our intimate time together. If* you will read The Song of Solomon *out loud to Me every day,*

1

I will show you where you are in your walk with Me. I will so change you, you will not even recognize yourself not many days from now."

Immediately I opened my Bible to The Song of Solomon and began to read out loud to Him.

Solomon's Song of Songs. Beloved. Let him kiss me with the kisses of his mouth—for your love is more delightful than wine (1:1-2).

He began this process of transformation with me 12 years ago. Now He has asked me to share with *you* what He has taught me: how you too can have this same wonderful intimate walk with our Lord through worship and study through The Song of Solomon. He loves you so much and He wants all of us, His Bride, to fall madly and passionately in Love with Him. This book describes the stages He shared with me to teach me how to achieve the deepest intimacy with Him, our Holy Lord, our precious Lord Jesus by living (not just visiting) in His Holy of Holies continually. If you hunger and thirst to know Him, then this book has been written *just* for you!

As you read The Song of Solomon out loud, you will draw closer to Him as you sense His nearness. It is here where you will begin to ask Him questions as you read, i.e., The Song of Solomon 1:7 (rest for His sheep). "Lord, You said there is rest for your sheep. How do I find this rest?" As you read, He will show you the answer to your question; you will find this rest in His secret place because He is there. It is there in His secret chambers where you will find and experience this wonderful gentle

2

peace, a stillness which brings tranquility to your inner man, quiet to your emotions, clarity to your mind, and a time of refreshment for your body.

This secret place is a very special holy suite or chamber in the spirit realm, not in the physical realm. It is here in this secret place where you will come to worship Him. It is here in His holy chambers (or Holy of Holies) where your thirst for intimacy with Him will be made complete over time.

Sweet friend, how do you fall in love with our precious, holy Lord? Let me take you on a journey of love through select verses of The Song of Solomon. And at the end of this journey you too will know how to fall in love with our beautiful Lord and Saviour, King Jesus, as He taught me.

Let him kiss me with the kisses of his mouth for your love is more delightful than wine (Song of Sol. 1:2)

"Lord, how do you kiss me with your kisses? You are Spirit. I live in a natural, physical body. Please show me." And He did.

But along with this came something which I did not know even existed: Transformation—I was transformed from the natural man into the spiritual man; then I began the process of being changed into His image and likeness over a period of time, for now and throughout eternity.

Every day as I read to Him The Song of Solomon *out loud with no distractions*, I drew closer to Him. As I drew closer to Him, He drew me into His Holy of Holies, His secret place and there we would meet together, just He and I, face to face. As I worshipped Him in His secret place, I sensed His love more and more. He is calling us to choose to step out of our comfort zone and shake off complacency. This is why He asks us to "arise" ("get up and go"). Come with Him into "His secret chambers" (Song of Sol. 1:4). It is in this place where we worship and adore Him from our hearts.

Pleasing is the fragrance of your perfumes (Song of Sol. 1:3a).

It is this perfume of love that is so intoxicating to us. His fragrance is so gentle and kind and loving; it is this love that draws us to His chambers—His secret chambers. As He pours out this divine love on us as we take the time to come into His secret chambers, He then reveals to us *how pleased* He is with our commitment to worship Him through reading The Song of Solomon.

When we worship Him from our hearts, we will sense His quiet pleasure with us, His precious children. He loves us so much and longs for time alone with us so He can impart to us more of Himself—His sweetness, His kindness, His compassion, and His Love. It is wonderful to sense His sweetness.

And his banner over me is love (Song of Sol. 2:4b).

As He covers us with His protection, we will feel so cherished!

One of my most favorite scriptures in the Bible is the

following: "With joy you will draw water from the wells of salvation" (Isaiah 12:3). Every time I read this verse, my heart leaps!

As we worship, the more water of life comes forth from within us and the more His Life (the wells of salvation) flows from within us, the more we will want to worship Him. Worship is such a privilege—to worship the King of Kings…to come into His very presence…to have tears gently flowing down our faces because we love Him so and sense His nearness, even closer than the next breath we breathe. Oh, what *joy*!

He loves it when we worship Him. What does it mean to worship Him? It means to love Him with our whole heart and all that is within us. "Praise the Lord O my soul, all my inmost being praise his holy name" (Psalm 103:1). It means to seek His face above all else; to desire to spend time in His Presence, *alone* with *Him* in His secret place, His Holy of Holies, as He teaches us His truths; to sing to Him and tell Him how much we adore Him; and to let Him speak to our hearts as we listen to His still, quiet voice. It means also that we need to create an atmosphere where He feels welcome, for example, to have worship music playing in the background for part of the time or our sweet voices lifted on high to Him in song. He is so holy and loves us. He is special!

As we worship Him, He rewards us with His presence. He loves it when we worship Him just because…. Just because why? Just because He's so precious…just because He's so wonderful…just because He is our beautiful Saviour…just because He is God the Almighty, and Jesus is His name!

When we worship Him, we are saying, "Lord, You are so wonderful, and we just want to be with You. We thank You for Your *presents,* but we desire a billion times more Your *presence!* I love You." Our Lord loves it when we *show* Him how much we adore Him.

As we read out loud (He specifically said *"out loud"*) The Song of Solomon every day, once a day will not be enough for us. This book is so precious. As we come to know Him in a deeper way, we will "eat" His Word (Jesus is the Bread of Life [John 6:35a]). We will not be able to get enough of this book, for our spirit-man cries out for our beloved Bridegroom!

As we worship Him while we read out loud, He will show us where we are in our walk with Him. We will have such joy as we worship Him through His book, *The Song of Solomon*, written with His beloved Bride in mind. He loves us!

Over time, we will realize through worship that we have wealth beyond measure residing in us. It is this well within us, this reservoir within which are all the true riches (peace, joy, etc.). It is this well we touch as we worship and cross over to His faith side. It is this well which is on the other side of the "season of surrender." There we will lack nothing! Let's worship Him! He loves us! "Precious Lord! We love You!"

New light will flood our minds (His revelation knowledge), and this truth will bring soundness to our being. At first we will see tiny seeds in the form of peace, kindness, etc. from all the hours, days, weeks, and months of worship. We will come to this great revelation that the master key to the abundant life in Christ Jesus is worship! This key brings us into His holy chambers reserved only for our precious Bridegroom and His beautiful Bride—us!

As we worship Him, we become renewed, with His love covering us. Our minds become clear of all outside influences as we shut out everyone and everything else in this special holy place of intimacy with our Lord—just He and us in His Holy of Holies, His secret place. As we worship Him in intimacy, we will throw off the shackles of being people pleasers; He, in turn, will show us how to become a heavenly Father pleaser. He loves us and knows so long as we are *afraid* of what people think, we will never be free to be who He created us to be—His own beautiful cherished children. As we worship, we become strong spiritually, mentally, emotionally, and physically. For as we worship Him intimately, we will discover the balm of Gilead is worship.

As we worship, we draw closer to Him and He draws us closer to Himself. He shares His secrets with us and reveals His Word to us in ways He never has done before. Worship teaches us to run after Him with abandoned hearts of deepest love for this One whom we adore...this One who shows such kindness to us...this One who is ever so patient with us...this One whose beautiful face we seek daily.

The Lord will reveal to us glimpses of our incredible future, as we worship Him and study His Word. He has a specific Word just for us and will deliver it to us as we draw closer to Him. When we hunger after Him, He will fill us. He loves us. His heart's desire is to *give us the abundant life in Christ* with peace, joy, love, and laughter. Yes, it is available to us. We will discover it as we continue on this most exciting life-transforming journey.

We will come face to face with the One who has our very own best interests at heart. He loves us!

As we worship, our trust in Him is being built up, precept upon precept, line upon line (Is. 28:13a KJV).

We will know all He wants for us is His very best. We will know and experience His protection for us. He hides us in Himself and will even carry us at times, as a shepherd does for one of his little ones—a lost and afraid little sheep. Our Shepherd is right there holding us and speaking gently to us. He loves us.

You have experienced all this through:

Reading The Song of Solomon
Out loud
To Him
Every day
In His secret place
With no distractions!

"Come, let us worship Him! Precious Lord, we adore You!"

Intimate worship is the key to His gentle, holy heart. As we leave His Holy of Holies after having worshiped Him (for at this time we do not yet live there, we are still only visitors invited in by the King) and return to our families, friends, etc., they will eventually notice a softness, a graciousness to us that was not there before. Because each day we spend time alone with Him as His intimate worshippers, we leave with more of His love in and upon us. In turn we will love our families, friends, etc. with His divine love more and more each and every day. Oh, He is so precious! Worship is the key to life. The key to His heart is the key to life.

As we worship our Lord, His Word will become flesh to us. What does that mean?

I am my lover's and my lover is mine (Song of Sol. 6:3a).

Our Lord is the Living Word, and as we worship Him and partake of His Word, the truth that He is our Beloved will enter into our spirit-man and become a part of us. This Word, His Word, will then become truth to us in our inner man. We will know we are His beloved and He is ours. That truth will reverberate in our spirit and we will be filled with joy!

My lover is to me a cluster of henna blossoms from the vineyards of En Gedi (Song of Sol. 1:14).

The fragrance of our Lord is tangible. We can "taste" (partake of) His special fragrance—the fragrance of love, joy, peace, and gentleness as we worship Him.

Have you ever entered a home and just as you stepped inside you could "taste," i.e., sense that "Love is spoken here"? There is a peace and a gentleness reflecting His character through this couple who are the owners of the home. His fragrance (like a cluster of henna blossoms) is present in that home. This is His fragrance which will be imparted to us as we worship Him. His fragrance will permeate our homes and be a special perfume no perfumer can duplicate!

Taste and see that the Lord is good, blessed is the man who takes refuge in him (Psalm 34:8).

We are His beloved! Worship Him as His beloved intimate worshipper!

When we come into His sweet presence, we begin to feel secure and comfortable with Him. Because we now feel relaxed and restful in His presence, He sees this is good and that we are now ready to enter into the next step: trust. We learn how to trust Him as we choose to place more and more of ourselves into His safekeeping.

And am convinced that he is able to guard what I have entrusted to him for that day (2 Timothy 1:12b).

Step 2

Birth of Trust

All night long on my bed I looked for the one my heart loves; I looked for him but did not find Him (Song of Sol. 3:1).

During the night many times like a young child we want reassurance that our daddy is still there. When we don't sense God's presence, is He still there? Yes. When we can't seem to make contact with Him, is He still there? Yes. It is during this time when He wants us to pursue Him even though we don't sense His presence. "And without faith it is impossible to please God" (Heb. 11:6a).

It is at this time He begins to wean us from the knowledge we receive from our senses over to His realm, the faith realm. As we continue daily in worship through *The Song of Solomon*, without any outward evidence of His Presence, at some point He will reward us for our diligence and once again we will sense His unmistakable sweet presence.

> *Scarcely had I passed them when I found the one my heart loves; I held him and would not let him go till I had brought him to my mother's house, to the room of the one who conceived me (Song of Sol. 3:4).*

Our Lord wants consistency and diligence from us, both of which bring great rewards from Him.

As children learn to trust their parents, we will learn to trust our Lord. How? When a baby cries, a loving father will pick her up, cuddle her, and reassure her of his love for her. So it is with our heavenly Lord. As we have our needs met by Him and He cuddles us and we feel His warmth around us, we will come to reach out to Him more and more and see that He is kind, gentle, and loving even while correcting us, when necessary.

We will experience this as we read *The Song of Solomon*. He loves us and will never leave us. He will always protect us and provide for us. After we have left His secret place, He will also place us in situations where we will not be victorious unless He acts on our behalf. He will undergird us and cause us to triumph, and once again, our trust in Him grows. He does this as we worship Him daily.

As we also study His Word, our faith is being built up little by little. As we come to know Him through The Song of Solomon more and more each day, we will come to *know* beyond a shadow of a doubt that He is trustworthy. We can only trust someone if we know him/her. He wants us to see He loves us and has us on His heart at all times. The more we come to *know* Him, the more we will come to *trust* Him. We will experience for ourselves His precious love, kindness, and patience. This, in turn, causes us to trust Him even more.

We have become a beautiful worshipper from worshipping Him through The Song of Solomon.

When He draws us into His secret place we learn how absolutely trustworthy He is. He told us how beautiful we are.

How beautiful you are, my darling! (Song of Sol. 1:15).

And his banner over me is love (Song of Sol. 2:4b).

He calls us His darling! He covers us with His Love. He protects us as His cherished one. He does this and so much more.

Sweet friend, we can learn to develop our trust and our confidence in Him in the secret place through The Song of Solomon. This (trusting in Him) is a prerequisite before He can begin the process of transformation in us.

In the natural when we were children learning to swim, we only followed the guidance of our swimming coaches after we had developed trust in them and knew without a doubt they would not let us drown. Our Lord will always save us. He will never ever let us drown—not in the water...not in grief...not in sorrow...not in despair…not in fear. Oh no! He loves us and will always be there for us! We are His precious children.

We are now ready to go forward. In the next step we will learn how to clearly hear His sweet voice and discern it from all others.

Step 3

Learning to Hear His Voice

His voice will become more and more clear to us in our spirit-man. We are coming to know Him, to know His voice by the quickening we perceive in our spirit-man when He speaks to us. After we have heard His voice over and over, we will know when it is He who is speaking to us. "I know my sheep and my sheep know me" (John 10:14b).

Sweet friend, as we sit at His feet and worship Him through *The Song of Solomon read out loud to Him every day in His secret place with no distractions*, our Heavenly Father sees our commitment, diligence, and effort to obey Him and will reward us every time. He loves us. He knows we have not traveled this road before, and He also knows us through and through. He created us and loves us and knows just how to encourage us through His kindness and His words of "get up and go" (said to me at least one million times by our Heavenly

Father as I stepped out on faith). I did not know anyone nor could I find a book by anyone who had traveled this same road of The Song of Solomon. If I had had somebody who could have shared these steps with me, it would have helped me greatly. I did not know what was happening! I had no clue; I just held His Hand and never let go. (It was only years later that He brought me to a precious book on this subject to affirm my experience. He had kept it hidden from me until I had completed His full plan for my destiny.)[1]

Our Father was so kind and gentle yet firm ("get up and go"). He wanted me to get out of my comfort zone and step out in faith.

Sweet friend, He wants us to see that He won't just pull us up from where we are and say to us, "I am God, and it's time for a change!" No! One thousand times no! He will only act on our behalf if we allow Him. Our precious Father is not the bully of the playground. He will work with us and proceed at our pace. He is *not* in a hurry and desires the best for us. We do not need to fear that He will push us into anything. No! Pushing and shoving are *not* part of His character. Leading and guiding are—that is why it is so important that we *know* His voice.

He cannot lead us until we are ready to follow. We cannot follow Him unless we know Whom we are following!

He will cheer us on; He's on our team! When we step out in faith, we hear Him say, "Good for you, you did it. I knew you could!" in the same way we speak to our children. We are His precious children. He loves us. His encouragement will cause us to move ahead toward our goal. Trust Him. He loves us! He is kind, gentle, and loving; He is precious.

How gentle His voice sounds to those who *obey* Him even while He corrects them. He speaks with authority but always in a kind manner to those who are quick to hear *and* to obey His voice.

As we worship Him through *The Song of Solomon read out loud to Him every day in His secret place with no distractions* and study His Word, our spirit-man becomes more and more open to hearing His sweet voice. As we come to know His voice in deeper and deeper ways, He will then lead us ever more into His will while simultaneously revealing to us His plans for our future, a future which is on the other side of our obedience (though as yet unseen by our natural eyes).

His voice will become more and more familiar as we worship, study His Word, and sit at His feet. We will discover His voice is precious and we will recognize His special qualities.

Our Lord can speak in a whisper (or as loud as a thunderstorm if we are in danger).

His voice may convict us but never condemn us.

His voice will always encourage us, never discourage us.

His voice will always speak the truth.

His voice will speak life, not death to us.

His voice will lift us up, not tear us down.

His voice will speak hope to us, never despair.

His voice will speak love to us, not hate.

His voice will speak victory to us, not defeat.
His voice will always lead us in triumph!

At first, we seek His face and see Him but as through a veil. When we do see Him for the first time, we will know Him for we will have heard His sweet voice whispering to us for so long. And we will recognize His voice when we finally see Him face to face. Our Lord will *not* be a stranger to us for we will recognize His "cooing" to us as He has done for years.

The cooing of doves is heard in our land (Song of Sol. 2:12b).

As we worship in His Holy of Holies, we will come to better know the sound of His sweet voice. As we discover how He sounds, then after a time He can begin to lead us more and more—just by His still, small voice. That precious voice—Mary recognized it when Jesus called to her and said gently, with all the love He had for her, "Mary!" and she *knew* it was Jesus on Resurrection Day.

His voice is so gentle, loving, and kind. He will speak our names as we *worship Him by reading The Song of Solomon out loud to Him every day in His secret place with no distractions.* He longs for us! He created us for Himself! We are beautiful to Him! We are precious to Him!

Let's worship Him now. "Precious Lord Jesus, we adore You. Please draw us ever closer to you in your secret place. Thank You. In Jesus' name, Amen."

When we are able to hear His voice clearly, He is ready to bring us to the next step: uprooting the "little foxes" (those things [for example, anger, unforgiveness, haughtiness] which hold us captive to the enemy) and exchanging them for more of Him. Much of this will take place as we continue to worship Him in His secret place.

[1] *Song of the Bride,* Jeanne Guyon, The Seed Sowers Christian Books Publishing House.

Step 4

Uprooting the "Little Foxes"

As He begins to show us "little foxes" which are within us and if left there will cause our destruction, He also asks our permission to remove them.

Catch for us the foxes, the little foxes that ruin our vineyards, our vineyards that are in bloom (Song of Sol. 2:15).

In my case one little fox was haughtiness. One day, after our worship time was over and I had left His secret place, I found myself in a situation where I had the opportunity to exhibit either humility or haughtiness. I chose haughtiness. The split second I did, immediately He said these words to my heart, loud and clear: *"haughty spirit."* I fell on my knees and repented as I said, "Yes, Lord, I see it!" (I didn't even know I had a haughty spirit.) "Please remove it."

When He removed the spirit of haughtiness from me, there was more room for Him to dwell in me. As He showed me other little foxes He wanted to remove from me, He filled me with His character and His holiness as He removed them from my life. As He removed one little fox from me, He would replace it with a quality of His nature; for example, when He removed haughtiness from me, He replaced it with meekness. He replaced judgmentalness with acceptance of another and anxiety with peace. All this changing happened little by little. One little fox uprooted and cut off at its roots, was exchanged for one attribute of His character. We exchange the bondage of the little foxes (one aspect of the old Adamic Nature) *for more of Him—His divine nature*.

He is healing.
He is life.
He is provision.
He is patience.

Our Lord is *all* this and more! So much more. As you allow Him to remove from you anger, He can replace it with peace. The following are other things He replaces in our lives with attributes of His character.

Sadness/grief	Joy
Harshness	Gentleness
Dissatisfaction	Contentment
Lack of self-worth	His worth
Lack of identity	His Identity
No power	His divine power
No authority	His authority

He rewards us for being willing to go through each season. As we go through the "season of surrender," we

21

begin to give up more and more little foxes.

At the beginning of this "journey of love," each day I would come into His secret chambers and read to Him The Song of Solomon. As I worshipped Him and sensed His closeness, He would again show me another little fox He had chosen to remove from my life with my permission, this time the little fox of unforgiveness. Shortly thereafter I was deeply wounded emotionally by a friend. He showed me how to deal with unforgiveness His way. Instead of denying the hurt, He invited me to come to Him, tell Him all about it as His child, and allow Him to heal my wounded heart with His love. This way I have not "stuffed and denied the hurt." I have not kept it inside nor denied the pain. Instead, I have come to Him, acknowledged the pain, and allowed Him to heal me.

Now, between His healing of my heart and the manifestation of that healing there is a delay because it is a *process*. Because the wound from my friend was very deep, I would go to Him every day and say, "Lord, I know You have healed me, yet I still *feel* pain." (Feelings are feelings and they are valid.) I asked Him, "Now would you please fill me with more of You for that one who hurt me because You are love?"

Over a period of time, as He filled me each day with more and more of Himself, His love, as I *worshipped Him through The Song of Solomon*, the pain would lessen until one day *my feelings and my actions were one and the same*. When I saw that person later, I had no animosity and could genuinely hug her since now I had the manifestation of my *choice* to forgive.

milk and honey are under your tongue (Song of Sol. 4:11a).

This scripture had now become a physical reality in my life.

He will place us in situation after situation until we come to the point whereby we are truly quick to forgive because we have come to see His love far surpasses "the luxury" (the words He said to me) of unforgiveness. It delights our Lord's heart each time we choose Him over our "rights."

Over time, the Lord did this with all the little foxes one by one by one in my life . Do we give them up willingly? Not usually. But as He takes us into His secret chambers, He rewards us with more of Himself each time He sees our willingness to give up one more "little fox."

Before we were born-again, we had no power to overcome the enemy; he is *merciless*! When we became born again, his power was broken over us through the Cross—the precious Blood of Jesus. It is only then that we can have power over the enemy. But he (Satan) hides that fact from us for he knows if he can keep us ignorant of our position in Christ as a new creation—free from his torment *legally*—then we are still his captives. But once we find out he is no longer our master, he knows his days are over with us as his captives because we can finally be set free from the little foxes and other aspects of the Adamic nature.

Is there a price? Yes! Our freedom cost Jesus His own precious Blood; He died not for His own freedom but for ours. He longs to see His beautiful Bride, the one for whom He died, set free from all the power of the enemy. The enemy has *no* power over the new creation unless we give it to him: 1) through ignorance or 2) purposely inviting him into our lives through continuing to live by the natural man (and entertain the little foxes).

Our Lord wants to set us free from the old "us" and He will during this season of surrender *if* we allow Him. And if we do, we will become the happiest, most joyful people on earth! We will love others through His divine, supernatural love flowing through us!

Our Lord is precious. He loves us and knows that only as He is given free reign in us to come against Satan and his "thugs" can we be fully protected and free.

As we give up more and more "little foxes," the enemy's hold on us becomes weaker and weaker. Glory to God forever! We can live in victory!

When we became born again, Jesus came into our hearts, but we were still filled with many vestiges of the old Adamic nature, e.g., anger, strife, unforgiveness, etc. It is these little foxes which our Lord is working to remove from our lives. Before we were born again, even though we tried to distance ourselves from anger, etc., it did not work. We need His power which is now available to us as His children through the mighty anointing of the sweet Holy Spirit (Acts 2:4) to come against the enemy and all his works. It is only the Blood of Jesus that empowers us to come against Satan. "They overcame him by the blood of the Lamb and by the word of their testimony" (Rev. 12:11a).

Our Lord knows that so long as we allow the little

foxes (anger, jealousy, envy, unforgiveness, etc.) to dominate us, we are an absolute slave to that spirit(s). We are controlled rather than controlling the situation. For when we allow those things in our lives, we open the door to the enemy. Legally, we have given him the right to force us to become his slaves.

and that they will come to their senses and escape from the trap of the devil, who has taken them captive to do his will (2 Timothy 2:26).

Our King wants the best for us. He is our wise and loving Lord. His desire is for us to become the person He envisioned when He created us. In the following verse the Lover (our Lord) is speaking:

I raised thee up under the apple tree: there thy mother brought thee forth: there she brought thee forth that bare thee (Song of Sol. 8:5b KJV).

We were *not* an afterthought decided by a man and a woman. No. Our Lord Himself caused us to be conceived. We are His "forethought," not a couple's afterthought. Isn't that wonderful? To think He planned our conception all along! So it is this person in Christ whom He is trying to unveil now to us, the new person, the one without flaw.

All beautiful you are my darling; there is no flaw in you (Song of Sol. 4:7).

How do we go from being the natural man with the old Adamic nature, that creation which was cursed and done away with (destroyed in Christ Jesus through the Cross) to become the spiritual man in Christ Jesus? First, we become born again. When this happens, we immediately pass out of the kingdom of darkness into the Kingdom of His beloved Son, the Lord Jesus Christ (Romans 10:9-10). At this time our spirit-man becomes born again, but we still have all the destructive little foxes attached to us by their roots.

Second, we need to ask Him to fill us with His Holy Spirit to come *up and on* (upon) us (Acts 2:4) so we may have *His power* to go through the process—the process of transformation. How does being transformed from the natural man into the spiritual man occur?

As our minds become renewed with the Word of God, we begin to see things as He sees them. We begin to see the ugliness of gossip, jealousy, anger, and bitterness which are within us and attached by their roots to us as part of the old Adamic destructive nature. As we begin to see these things He shows us they are *not* a part of the new creation and must be uprooted from our lives one at a time. Because we now see with His eyes, we agree with Him and want them all to be uprooted, immediately! But He does not do this. Why? Because first we could not handle it, neither physically nor emotionally. Secondly, during this time He is developing patience in us. As He begins to show us the old person (weighed down with the destructive forces of jealousy, anger, bitterness) as we have never seen ourselves before, He also shows us glimpses of the new person we can become *in Him* (who is sweet, kind, gentle), the one He will bring forth in due time if we continue to allow Him to transform us. He shows us all this as we come into *His secret place and worship Him*. He is gentle and loves us. Here in this secret place He will show us the next little fox He wants to remove from our lives.

When we are well into the process of being set free from the *roots* of anger, bitterness, jealousy, unforgiveness, etc., He rewards us with more and more of His manifest sweet presence. He does this each time we obey Him and allow Him to rip out all the little foxes (He knows how hard it is for us), one by one by one.

During this time, He will tenderly hold us as His precious child. He will speak words of comfort to us and tell us He loves us and accepts us just as we are. Because He loves us so much, He will not leave us as we are, *but* He will begin the process of transformation from the natural man into the spiritual man, with our permission. What a glorious future He has for us. Let's sing out His beautiful name—Jesus—with all the love we feel for Him. He is so precious! He will reveal Himself to us in a special way. He is holy, pure and gentle. Let's ask Him to impart His holiness, purity, and gentleness (these characteristics of His character) to us. He loves to answer such a prayer! "Lord Jesus, would You please do this for us? Thank You, precious Lord. In Jesus' Name, Amen."

As we are being divested from the little foxes one by one, we will come to know a greater degree of freedom in our lives. We will be less controlling for now we are more under the control of the sweet Holy Spirit. We will be less judgmental for now we are beginning to see with His eyes of love.

Each day He brings us into His secret chambers and

shows us more and more of His plan—His wonderful plan for our lives. Though it is still in the future, we know for a certainty it will come to pass. We have developed our trust in Him (for to know Him is to trust Him) as we have *worshipped Him through The Song of Solomon.*

As He sees our perseverance along the way, He will have sweet surprises for us. We will also experience divine appointments, miracles, and a fruitful life—all this even before we are transformed.

I delight to sit in his shade and his fruit is sweet to my taste (Song of Sol. 2:3).

All these are His rewards for our willingness to change.

He longs for us. He loves us and has chosen us for His Bride. We are precious to Him. "Draw nigh to God and he will draw nigh to you" (James 4:8 KJV).

If we were the only people on earth who ever would have received Jesus, He would have died just for us!

How lovely is our holy, beautiful Lord. Let's tell Him how much we love Him. "Jesus, Precious, we love You!"

In these Last Days, those who cherish Him and are willing to go through full surrender are going to walk in His glory. "Now if we died with Christ, we believe that we now will live with Him" (Romans 6:8). He is searching throughout the earth for those who are willing to go through His training camp (the season of *total* surrender) and emerge transformed.

All beautiful you are, my darling, there is no flaw in you (Song of Sol. 4:7).

Uprooting the "Little Foxes"

Like a lily among thorns is my darling among the maidens (Song of Sol. 2:2).

Have you ever been to a social gathering when as you walked around the room you heard one group of people who were jealous of another group gossiping about them? These are "thorns" to our Lord. But us? We are now different from the others. We have become His darling among the thorns. Why?

Because we are in the process of exchanging the little foxes which are within us for more of Him during the "season of total surrender," the very first stage to be taken if we desire the deepest intimacy with our holy Lord. At this time He is asking you to allow Him to rip out one little fox from your life. Let's take jealousy for example. Jealousy leads to gossip—neither of which is pleasing to our Lord. This little fox must be pulled up by its roots and die, leaving more room for our Lord to live in us. We are clothed with His grace (divine favor, His beauty) in many areas of our lives at this time. We are so pleasing to Him that we are becoming His beautiful lily.

My lover is mine and I am His; He browses among the lilies (Song of Sol. 2:16).

At this point, we are in the first stage of fruit bearing. This is the early fruit referred to in The Song of Solomon 2:13a: "The fig tree forms its early fruit." As we continue to go through surrender, our "fruit" will become more and more evident as we relinquish more and more of the little foxes to Him.

Where does He browse? Among the lilies—those who

are allowing Him to transform them through surrender (giving up all the little foxes). Does He browse among the thorns (i.e., those who *choose* to live in anger, strife, etc.)? No! No one wants to be pricked by thorns! Our Lord delights in being among the lilies.

We are one of His precious lilies if we continue to allow Him by the power of His sweet Holy Spirit to uproot the little foxes from our lives. He is beautiful and is making us more and more beautiful each day with His own beauty. Let's thank Him! "Thank You, precious Lord Jesus. We love you."

I am the rose of Sharon, and the lily of the valleys (Song of Sol. 2:1 KJV).

The Lover is speaking: He alone is the Rose of Sharon! How do I know it is our Lord who is speaking? I've experienced His incredible rose fragrance. One day as I walked into the lobby of a condominium I immediately detected the fragrance of roses—the fragrance was everywhere—the floors and walls seemed to be permeated with that luscious fragrance, yet not a flower nor petal was anywhere. When I returned to my car, the same fragrance was there, yet there were no roses in my car either. As I drove home, He spoke to me in my spirit-man. I have experienced this same indescribable fragrance one other time during these past 12 years. (This occurred shortly after I had begun my study of The Song of Solomon.)

What is the primary characteristic of the lily? Purity. Our Lord is pure and He will exchange a little fox (impurity/uncleanness) in us for His purity. He will do this as we *worship Him.*

He will stay with us and help us break free from the effects of the old Adamic nature (anger, strife, etc.).

As we go forward in our new walk of genuine intimacy with our Lord, we will begin to see one bondage after another fall away from us while at the same time we will draw ever closer to Him through quality worship (through The Song of Solomon and study of His Word).

One day in our journey as we progress more and more and never give up, we will have increased understanding, and the truth of His Word will no longer be obscured by shadows.

Until the day breaks and the shadows flee (Song of Sol. 2:17).

I looked for the one my heart loves; I looked for him but did not find him (Song of Sol. 3:2b).

How do we search for Him? First, not with our intellects but with our hearts and our emotions. It is with our emotions we run after our Lord, not with our heads. He wants *heart*-felt passion. He wants to know we desire Him above all else.

It is as we worship Him from *our hearts* that we draw closer to Him. He doesn't just want our lip service; He wants our heart service. It is a diligent search—through days, weeks, months of worship and study of His Word. As we study His Word through *The Song of Solomon*, we will come to *know* (be intimately acquainted with) Him. He is the Living Word. As we allow His Word to become the deepest part of us, we will have a deeper revelation of *who He is.*

This is a search, which means we must dig deep and dig far. These truths are not on the surface but are found as we study (not skim through) His Word and put whatever truths He begins to show us into practice in our daily lives.

> *How beautiful you are, my darling. Oh how beautiful. Your eyes behind your veil are doves (Song of Sol. 4:1a).*

We are now beautiful to Him. Why? Because our eyes are now filled with His love, His compassion, and His kindness. How did our eyes, which before were filled with suspicion, haughtiness, fear, and anger, become so transformed that our Lord now calls them "dove's eyes"?

> *His eyes are like doves by the water streams washed in milk mounted like jewels (Song of Sol. 5:12).*

His dove's eyes are now becoming our eyes and are filled with forgiveness, mercy, peace, and gentleness because we have become intimate worshippers and students of His Word through *The Song of Solomon.*

As He speaks tenderly to us, He shares with us how delighted He is. We have allowed Him to remove all the little foxes of the old cursed Adamic nature by their roots (i.e., anger, bitterness, strife, etc.). This in turn has made more room for His perfume of love to fill us.

We have also learned He is so trustworthy. We now are able to discern His voice from all others. We are now ready for the next step: coming to the end of self (our plans, will, purposes versus His plans, will, and purposes for our lives).

Step 5

Coming to the End of Self (Old Nature)

Because our trust in Him has greatly increased, we now know His voice, and the little foxes (anger, bitterness, envy, etc.) which were within us have been fully uprooted and therefore destroyed, He has been able to bring us to the next step: coming to the end of self. This step puts our plans, will, purposes, dreams, and desires in opposition to His plans, His will, His purposes for *us*. How does He introduce us to this next step?

He may place two options in front of us: 1) His will versus 2) your will. For example: He might say to us: "It's time to move" 1) His Will. But we don't want to do it 2) (our will).

Each time there are two different options in front of me, I have learned to pray the following prayer first said by a well-known evangelist in the 1980s: "Lord, I have no will of my own in this situation. I only want Your divine will, plan, purpose for my life. Please show me; I don't know which option is Your choice for me." Then through His Word (undergirded by peace) and a series of circumstances, He will show us what His Will is. When we say "Yes, Lord" to His will and purpose for our lives and thus show Him we trust Him, this pleases Him. After we have obeyed Him by having done what He has asked us to do, then He will reward us for our obedience with a deeper level of His presence than we have known before.

Over a period of time, as we obey Him regarding His will versus our will, slowly, ever so slowly, His will *becomes* our will and His plans *become* our plans. The more we obey Him, the more He rewards our obedience with more of Himself.

During this process of transformation, much of it will take place in His secret chambers as we worship Him away from the gaze of others. A baby is conceived and develops in his or her mother's womb away from the eyes of others. Our new man's holy conception and development (transformation) also come about away from the eyes of others. This takes place in His secret chambers.

How? As we sit at His feet, He will speak tenderly to us. He will encourage us in our walk. He will always tell us how pleased He is with our progress (with choosing His will over ours, His plan not ours).

Lover speaking:

I went down to the grove of nut trees to look at the new growth in the valley (Song of Sol. 6:11a).

The "new growth" takes place "in the valley." Because it does, this paves the way for our future when He will bring us into our destiny.

Thy temples are like a piece of a pomegranate within thy locks (Song of Sol. 4:3b KJV).

Our (temples) mind has been renewed after we have spent hours and hours digging into His Word for "true riches" as well as hours and hours in His presence, i.e., in the presence of love as we worship. The combination of worship and the Word has brought about revelation knowledge unlike anything we have known before.

We no longer think the same way we did before. We now have His mind in us because of hours and hours of diligence on our part in His secret chambers and study of His Word. Our renewed minds have His wisdom for every situation and are clear and unencumbered. They are quick, sharp, and decisive. We are also choosing to do His Will more and more versus our own. His will is becoming our will.

As we read *The Song of Solomon out loud to Him every day in His secret chambers with no distractions*, we experience Him on a deeper level. That in itself causes us to be His willing student, ready to go through the process of transformation. He does the work, not through our will power, but His love power encouraging us, loving us, caring for us, protecting us, delighting Himself in us as He sees our heart's desire is to cooperate with Him in this season of total surrender.

He longs so much for us to receive and act on all He

has for us. And the more we allow Him to transform us, the more we will receive the abundant life He came to give us. He encourages us to stay with His plan for us when He calls us His darling.

Arise, come my darling, my beautiful one, come with me (Song of Sol. 2:13b).

To the degree we have made room for Him by being willing to die to our hopes, dreams, plans, and agenda, is to the degree we are now alive in Him to *His* hopes, dreams, and plans for us.

The horse is made ready for the day of battle, but victory rests with the Lord (Prov. 21:31).

Jesus loves us! He is so proud of us! We will not always be living in this season of total surrender. This day (season) of surrender is so short compared to the days (season) of joy, love and an incomparable life—His life *in us*. For the other side of total surrender is Resurrection Day forever! *We are almost there!*

"I will instruct you and teach you in the way you should go; I will counsel you and watch over you" (Psalm 32:8).

Oh sweet friend! Jesus loves us. He really does. We are precious to Him!

One day something will occur that we did not expect. It will bring excruciating pain to us emotionally to the point we could not have survived had He not held us and carried us during this time. We once again have two choices: surrender our "Isaac" on the altar and trust our

37

Lord (no sickness, no disease, nothing which comes to kill, steal and destroy; this is the enemy, not God). What I am referring to here is a special person, place or thing He has promised to us and He is now asking us to offer up to Him as our special supreme sacrifice.

Step 6

Final Sacrifice

Step 6a: Final Sacrifice Asked For

We draw ever deeper in Him as we continue to *Worship Him through The Song of Solomon read out loud to Him every day in His secret place with no distractions.* We are so passionately in love with Him and are almost at the top when we hear Him say "Come up higher." We willingly run after Him as we climb the hill higher and higher with Him.

Then when we reach it, He says there is another sacrifice. We need to offer up our Isaac. We must place this special, supreme sacrifice on the altar.

Nobody goes through the full transformation process without hearing that precious voice calling us to give up our Isaac!

"No, Lord, I can't. You promised me! I've been faithful to You all this time. No, Lord, I can't!"

Such excruciating pain is included in these final throes of death to "self."

No, Lord. Please, not that! And we cry from the depth of our spirit-man the same exact words Jesus said on His Cross. "My God! My God! Why have You forsaken me?" (Matt. 27:46b) Our cries are uncontrollable and the "wail" bursts forth from the depth of our being, our inner core. We have no control over the sound—it just comes!

Everything else He asked us to do we did—no questions—just followed where He led us. Sweet friend, He will never ever ask us to do something He did not have to do. No. His own precious Son had to give the supreme sacrifice, and He is God with no sin ever attached to Him! In order to *break* the *power* over *self* fully and completely, *self must die.* During this excruciatingly painful time, we will know Him and His Presence in a way we never have before. He knows the pain! Jesus died so He knows the pain. If it were not absolutely necessary, He would never have asked us to do it. He loves us!

But now, this one last final sacrifice (I did not know it was *the* final sacrifice at this time), I wrestled with Him over many days and cried the whole time day and night. My husband's death *broke* me (the enemy kills, *not God*). My final sacrifice years later (my new Isaac) offered, accepted, and completed, *freed* me. Because now s*elf* was fully and completely *destroyed. Dead* for now and for all eternity. "For he/she that is dead is freed from sin" (Rom. 6:7 KJV).

The following scripture became a physical reality at that moment in my life: "Who will rescue me from this body of death? Thanks be to God through Jesus Christ our Lord!" (Rom. 7:24b and 25a)

"But he who unites himself with the Lord is one with him in spirit" (1 Cor. 6:17). This became a reality *after* the final sacrifice. To be sure, we become one spirit with our Lord when we become born again. It is that oneness which is now being revealed more and more in deeper and deeper levels and throughout eternity, which took place in me after I had offered my final sacrifice.

Jesus wrestled with His Father's will for Him to go through the Cross experience and you will with yours.

Finally, after days and days of sobbing (the "wailing" part is over), you go to our Lord and sob out these words.

Step 6b: Final Sacrifice Offered

"Here is my Isaac. I place my Isaac on your altar. I love You, Lord, more than anyone or anything else."

That is the hardest thing you will ever, ever do in your life! He understands your pain.

Step 6c: Final Sacrifice Accepted

You know in your heart He is pleased although there is no outward evidence. It is a quick work!

Though my husband's death broke me, please know our heavenly Father is kind and loving and never ever breaks anyone—not through sickness, not through disease. No! Death is His enemy and He hates it. Because we live in the fallen Adamic nature, we are attached to the author of that nature, the enemy himself. He is the one who kills, steals, and destroys—not our kind, precious, beautiful Lord who died for us!

Our Father does *not* break us. No bone of Jesus' was

allowed to be broken on the Cross! "Not one of His bones will be broken (John 19:36b [further reference: Ex. 12:46]). Jesus came to redeem us. Not to break us but to *heal us*!

How does He heal us? By pulling us *up and out* from *living* in the fallen nature whose master is Satan. How? By causing us to be born again and *all* little foxes uprooted and *all* self (the old "you") annihilated by total surrender. Then we come under a new Master (Saviour). He is kind, gentle, loving, and healing. He cries when He sees how His children get hurt because they have not yet learned how to give up *all* "three parts" of the old and be transformed into all "three parts" of the new creation.

Years ago when one of our precious daughters was a little girl, she fell and broke her arm. I cried when the orthopedic surgeon said he would have to re-break the bone in order to line it up properly so it could heal perfectly. If I cried and I'm a human parent, how much more does our heavenly Father cry when we, His precious children, get hurt? He loves us. His Son died for us! No! Sweet friend, our God is loving and kind. He heals. *Never* will He hurt us, His precious children! He loves us.

Don't believe anybody who says He breaks us—no, He does *not*! "A bruised reed he will not break" (Is. 42:3a). *The fallen world* and the *sin nature and its effects cause* us to become broken. *Not our Lord!* Never! He heals us; He does *not break* us. He uses broken vessels, you (and me), broken by the *enemy, not by our Lord Jesus*. He heals us and makes us whole! He loves us. We are precious!

The old must die! It already has spiritually on the Cross of Jesus. Now it must die in the physical realm in us. Its death in the spiritual realm (already a "done deal") is now being enforced in the natural realm. The old must *die* before the "three-part" new man fully and completely *transformed* can begin to be *changed* into His image and likeness from glory to glory for now and for all eternity. This is why the Lord wants to set us free completely from Satan's grip. This is why He is revealing this awesome revelation to us in these Last Days—how to become free and then stay free.

We inadvertently give Satan the right to be in our lives through our attachment to the little foxes and to the old nature—the Adamic nature (Jesus died a horrible death because of those little foxes).

Soon we will hear Him say "It is finished!"

PART I: TOTAL SURRENDER

Step 7

Final Sacrifice Completed Forever

We will hear Him roar, *"It is finished!"* Glory to God! He is alive *in us* (the new us, the transformed us), fully and completely living and breathing through every part of us, that is, "Christ in us, the hope of glory" (Col. 1:27).

How did we arrive here at such an awesome place? Totally free from Satan? Let's review.

1) Our spirit-man became born again.
2) All little foxes (destructive "termites") were pulled up by their roots, severed/cut off from us, and therefore died.
3) Our fallen nature (Adam's) was totally annihilated when a megaton bomb blew it up and out of existence. What was that bomb? That bomb was the offering up by us of our supreme final sacrifice. This we were able to do through the power of the Holy Spirit and now we are

44

free from Satan's attachment to us through the old Adamic nature.
4) Soul (mind, will, emotions)
   a) Our minds have been renewed through studying the Word of God.
   b) Our will has been submitted to His. We are hiding our will inside His will voluntarily!
   c) Our emotions are now under His authority.
5) Body: our body now offered daily as a living sacrifice to Him, holy and acceptable to Him.
6) Self annihilated through our final sacrifice.

How can we stay free? Our Lord has a preventative program for us, His precious Bride, through which we can stay free. His preventative program to stay free is the following:

1. Worship Him daily (John 4:23)
2. Pray in other tongues (Acts 2:4)
3. Study His Word (2 Tim. 3:15)
4. Make a covenant with your eyes to allow no unclean thing before them (Ps. 101:3)
5. Think only on things that are lovely, pure and of good report (Phil. 4:8)
6. Look for ways to bless our Lord daily (1 Cor. 11:23)
7. Look for ways to bless others daily (Luke 4:18-19)
8. Be a tither (Mal. 3:8-10)
9. Be a giver (Luke 6:38)
10. Then "do" (2 Peter 1:1-11)
And you will not fall!

Can we still sin? Yes. If we take our submitted will out from its hiding place in Him, we can sin. But the moment we do, we will know it and just as quickly we will repent and slip our will right back inside His (He is our hiding place). We are *not* perfect. *He alone* in us (in our spirit-man) *is*! We (the "three-part" new creation) will be *changed* more and more and more into His beauty and loveliness for all eternity.

We will *know* His love in such a special way that 99% of the time as we are learning how to walk in this "three-part" new creation on this earth, we will choose Him over our "right." We will do everything and anything to keep growing in this *holy intimacy with our Lord*.

Sweet friends, this revelation is awesome. I can hardly write fast enough with my pen. To be sure those ministers who are highly anointed have already gone through total surrender and have offered up their Isaac (supreme, final sacrifice). There were others in the last century who also went through full surrender and were also deeply anointed. Why? Because it wasn't (isn't) the person (neither now nor then) but "*Christ* (in His divine nature *fully* and *completely* in their "three- part" new creation) in them the hope of glory" (Col. 1:27). Glory to our Lord forever! We are free. Please stay free in Him and for Him!

To be sure, this is *not* a new revelation. It is only new to us who now understand the steps needed to bring about total freedom from Satan and *stay* that way through a life lived in holy intimate relationship with our holy Lord forever. This happens only *after* our final sacrifice has been completed and His enemy's nature has been annihilated from us.

Though I am aware most people use the words "transformation" and "change" interchangeably, for the purpose of this book I am purposely using the word *"transformation"* to describe the process of the old "one-part' (born again) man into the "three-part" *new man* and *"change"* when referring to the "three-part" new creation (His Bride). This *change* into His image and likeness will go on forever and forever into eternity.

This *change* into His beauty and loveliness only comes about *after* we have offered our final sacrifice. Why do I call it the final sacrifice? Because this is the final sacrifice you will ever offer as a *one-part* (born again) *non*-transformed person. From now on, all sacrifices we offer (and there will be plenty from now until Jesus comes) will be offered by the new "three-part" transformed you. This "three-part" new creation is now fully attached and one with Him through His divine nature flowing through us. We are clothed with His glory. Resurrection Day is at hand! What joy it was to hear Him roar these words, "It is finished," after I had offered and He had accepted my final supreme sacrifice.

Step 8

Resurrection Day

Oh, hallelujah! It is finished! at this point in our journey He reveals everything to us, the "three-part" new creation. He rewards us now for the pain we have endured.

When we emerge a "three-part" new creation, all things have become new. We are now the beautiful ones for whom He planned when we were conceived in our mother's womb. Our old selves were marred by sin and its effects, but now we are full of love, life, and laughter.

Love because we are now hidden in Christ; Christ in *us,* not us, but Christ in *you* (us) the hope of glory (Col. 1:27). This new "us" at this time has never known pain, sadness, sorrow and has never before been seen on this earth.

Now this light from within us is no longer just a little light that shines, but He has taken up full residence in us and shines fully through us since now *Christ* is in us.

Oh, He's so precious! Now we run after Him because

we have discovered no matter how much He reveals Himself to us in His secret place, there is always more to know—so much more—and it will take all eternity to really, really know Him. "Oh how precious, sweet Lord, You are."

This new "you" is the one Jesus saw in your mother's womb, without spot or wrinkle. This new "you" is the real "you."

This person is being unveiled to us little by little, and we love what we see—and so do others for it is now Christ in *you* (us) whom people see. Christ in us, not just us alone but "*Christ* in you (us) the hope of glory" (Col. 1:27).

This season, the "three-part" new creation is one with great fruitfulness. We are now undergirded with His patience, see with His eyes of love, and touch with His hands of compassion. We are encompassed about with Him on every side.

It is His sweetness people see in you.

It is His beauty people see in you.

And because we love Him, we always give Him the praise and glory when people try to praise us.

We are now His trophy which He proudly displays to the world. We bring great joy to His precious heart each and every day.

This is the new "three part" you:

1) Spirit born again.
2) Soul
   a) mind—totally renewed through the Word of God, now having the mind of Christ.
   b) will—voluntarily submitted to His.

   c) emotions—under His governorship, and the
little foxes uprooted and dead.
3) Body—alive unto God, offered as a living
sacrifice, holy and acceptable to Him *daily*.
Self—dead, annihilated through your final
completed sacrifice.

Our Lord is so precious, so beautiful and we have
fallen madly and passionately in Love with Him because:
We have read

The Song of Solomon

Out loud

to Him

Every day

In His secret place

With no distractions.

We have allowed Him to transform us. Now that we
are transformed into His "three-part" new creation, we
are allowing Him to *change* us into the beauty and loveliness of His only begotten Son, Jesus. He is the first
born Son of this loveliness which will grow brighter and
brighter in us throughout eternity.

The "three-part" old person is gone forever. The
"three-part" new person is the transformed "you" who is
being changed into His image and likeness forever. He
loves us so! The little foxes have been totally destroyed
and self has died completely. Our self attached to the
Adamic Nature was annihilated through the final sacrifice.

Our love is more pleasing to Him than the finest

wine and more fragrant to Him than the rarest perfume. The fragrance He is experiencing, which brings such delight to His heart, is His dwelling in us. He delights in our loving Him through our own unique personality, which He placed into us before we were conceived (our spiritual DNA). We are now His "three-part" transformed children, who are in the ongoing process of *being changed* more and more into the image and likeness of His precious Son Jesus for now and throughout eternity.

He has chosen us to be alive in this end time. No other generation has ever had the privilege He is giving to us. He trusts us to carry out His plan, His purpose and His will.

You anoint my head with oil; my cup overflows (Psalm 23:5b).

All beautiful you are, my darling; there is no flaw in you (Song of Sol. 4:7).

To those who through the righteousness of our God and Saviour Jesus Christ have received a faith as precious as ours: His divine power has given us everything we need for life and godliness through our knowledge of him who called us by his own glory and goodness. Through these he has given us his very great and precious promises so that through them you may participate in the divine nature and escape the corruption in the world caused by evil desires (2 Peter 1:1, 3-4).

We who have persevered have prevailed and now our hearts cry out with joy as we hear Him say how pleased He is with us. Today as we *worship Him through reading the Song of Solomon*, there is a greater depth in our intimacy with Him, a greater love for Him for unveiling to us the "three-part" real person in us. This is the one who is without flaw in Him. Oh, how we cry out to Him in thanksgiving for all He has done for us, and all the time He patiently took to lead and guide us into this glorious oneness with Himself.

We now live only for His pleasure—first, worshipping Him in His secret place and second, ministering His love to others, every day. He is the one who is so anointed, and who paid the price—the full price. Just as Jesus paid the full price, so have we paid the price because we want Him totally.

Remember at the very beginning of my love walk with Him He said to me, "*If* you will read out loud to Me the Song of Solomon every day with no distractions." "If" is a very big word! *If* I had not, He *would* not. For *if* I had not, He *could* have not.

It was only as I obeyed His instructions, even though I did not understand His plan, that he showed me what He wanted to remove from me and how to cooperate with Him. So *if* I had not, He could have not, for only as I *saw* these little foxes was He then able to uproot them and transform me. I was totally in denial about my real state, the state of the old "me," the old Adamic nature. So *if* I had not done what He had said, He never could have transformed me. I would have missed out on the purpose for my creation: to bring pleasure to the heart of My Father as His "three-part" *transformed* daughter with whom He is now beginning the on-going process of *change* for now and for all eternity into the loveliness of His Son Jesus.

After we have brought pleasure to Him through worship and study of His Word, then He draws us closer and closer to Himself and reveals how He wants to work through us.

We now become His eyes to see the searching heart who is looking for Him. We become His ears to hear one calling on His Name. We become His hands to tenderly love a child. We become His feet to bring His Gospel of Good News wherever He so directs.

The new "three-part" person is the new creation. At the very core of this new creation is the very essence of Christ Himself. For He is now fully *in* us and One with us. His very essence (love, joy, peace, and patience) manifests through us (Christ in you, not you, but "*Christ in you* the hope of glory" [Col. 1:27]). It is this One whom people now see in us. As they come close to us, they *feel* His love flowing and pulsating through us. They are drawn to us (*Christ in us*) like a magnet. For it is to this new person people run. The "old you" (one-part born again "you") was much like the world. They have "baggage" and we had "baggage." Ah! But the new person. . . that's a different story because we are free in Him. It is this new transformed person for whom people are desperately searching, because they see in you—Jesus.

Just as one cannot receive the mighty Baptism of the Holy Spirit with the evidence of speaking in other languages (Acts 2:4) unless one is born again, neither can one be *changed into* His image and likeness until he has been transformed. The old fallen destructive Adamic nature and its effects—the self and the little foxes of destructive works—must be annihilated in our physical being as we (in our old nature) have already been annihilated on the Cross of Jesus when He became that curse for us.

This is why the Church has been powerless for the last 2,000 years. We thought *transformation* and *change* were one and the same, the same mistake we had made in reference to: 1) the new birth and 2) the Baptism of the Holy Spirit. We did not realize one had to go through *full* surrender, *final* sacrifice, *and* the annihilation of self. Self (the destructive Adamic nature) must be dead *before* we can begin to change into His image and likeness. They are two separate actions.

Once transformation has taken place (your final sacrifice causing the *final annihilation* of self), then and only then will He begin the ongoing process of *change*. He will then begin to *change* us into His beauty and loveliness for all eternity. Glory to our Lord forever! This is awesome.

He is revealing this awesome revelation to His Church so He in us, not us alone, can show the world *finally* who Jesus really is! He is God—majestic and all-powerful! These truths only come about as we worship Him in His secret place.

The fallen nature, from which we are now free, originally tied His beloved mankind to Satan from Adam's fall until now. In this last generation before Jesus returns for

His Bride, it is this revelation (not new but hidden from most of us) which will enable His Church, His Bride to become the Army that Joel speaks about in Joel 2:10-11a:

> *Before them, the earth shakes, the sky trembles, the sun and moon are darkened and the stars no longer shine. The Lord thunders at the head of his Army.*

The "three-part" new you in Him is His awesome revelation in these last days.

Within this new creation, He has placed myriad gifts which we will soon have the joy of discovering. He loves us and placed these delights in us before we were even conceived. How precious is our Lord!

Step 9

Discovering His Gifts in Us

As we worshipped Him, He has taken delight in having revealed to us one gift He has placed in us before the foundation of the world. This wonderful discovery spurred us on to search for more gifts which are hidden within us. After having studied His Word in depth, we have come to see what we are passionate about. For one person it might be studying medicine, another fashion, another sports, another teaching, the law, or one of the arts such as singing, dancing, painting, or writing. You might be an author and not know it at this time. Another one might study to become a minister. There are so many passions and all of them wonderful. He placed that passion in us before we were even born—that is why we have to follow after our own heart. He gives us the desires of our heart after His desires have become our desires. It is He who causes conception of those desires (dreams) within us. It is we who must labor (travail) over those dreams until we bring them forth (birth them) in His timing. It is a process; never, never, never give up your God-conceived dreams.

Because we have remained faithful to Him, continuing to tithe and give, and have remained *thankful* for all He has given us, He, in turn, has prepared us in His training camp for the destiny He has for us. At this time, He begins to release our gifts from within us. All our gifts were there all the time, but remained hidden beneath the veil of the natural man. Now, we, the new creation can begin to blossom everywhere we go. And our gifts will come forth to bless others as well as ourselves. As our gifts come forth (including His beauty, His sweetness, His passion for your spouse, family, friends—i.e., His passion for life), we must be sure to give Him all the glory!

Our Lord said to me a number of years ago, "Helen, the beauty and sweetness people see in you is really *Me*!" "Yes, Lord!" Give Him the glory—all of it, all the time! It isn't you; it is *Christ in you* (the "three-part" new "you"—the hope of glory (Col. 1:27). He alone deserves all the glory and all the praise. Both belong to Him. Anything good people see in you is really God in you!

As His assignments for us enlarge, we must be sure to keep Him first and not allow ministering *for* Him to ever take the place of ministering *to* Him. If we make that mistake, we will lose His tangible, sweet, holy intimacy reserved only for His "three-part" transformed new creation Bride in His secret chambers. Nobody, no job, and no ministry ever should come before Him! He means what He says—no distractions. (He does not leave you but His tangible presence is only found in His Holy of Holies, reserved for the Bridegroom and His Bride.)

A word to the wise: In the very beginning of my love walk with God, the Lord specifically said "Read The Song of Solomon out loud to Me every day with *no distractions.*" This is what is referenced here in the Song of Solomon 3:1b: "I sought him, but I found him not" (KJV). If we allow distractions to occur during our holy intimate time in His secret place with Him every day as we read out loud to Him The Song of Solomon, then we are showing Him we neither cherish nor revere Him. When we begin to read The Song of Solomon out loud to Him the next time, we will *not* be able to enter into His Holy of Holies—the heavens will feel like brass! The Holy of Holies is His secret place. Though we may cry for Him with genuine tears, He still will *not* answer. This happened to me. Even after I had asked for His forgiveness for having allowed distractions during our intimate time together and cried because I had inadvertently hurt the One I adore (and He had forgiven me), it was a while before I again sensed His *tangible* presence. (He never left me, but His tangible presence was not made manifest at this time.)

His peace eventually opened the door as He once again invited me to come into His Holy of Holies which is reserved only for our Bridegroom and His Bride. This was at the very beginning of this precious love walk and I learned that He alone is in charge of His Holy of Holies, and it is a privilege to have been invited by Him into His secret place. Never take Him for granted! He is so pre-

cious! Choose your time wisely to have this special intimacy with our Lord. He will *not* allow *any distractions.*
It must be *uninterrupted time.* He must be *first.* Slow
down and worship Him because there is nothing more
important than worshipping Him!

We are like the mares of Pharaoh because we want to
jump into our destiny. We are chomping at the bit to be
fully released (like a race horse), but He does not want
us to sprint ahead of His timing.

He's releasing us more and more each day—effort-
lessly. We have done the preparation, now comes the ex-
hilaration, but we must be careful to put Him *first.* We
must not get ahead of Him. I promise you, no one else
will take your destiny because He has reserved it for
you. Slow down and let Him lead you, so that it will
occur not in your timing but His.

We might not be called to the ministry. That's fine.
My late husband, the man I adored, was an Ob-Gyn
physician. Each time his patients' babies were born, the
first hands to have touched those babies from heaven
were the hands of Jesus through my precious husband!
Isn't that just like our gentle, loving Lord? So we too
might be called to share our gifts in a very special way
though not as a pastor, evangelist, or prophet, but still
very much as someone ministering God's love through
our gifts in the wonderful destiny He has for us.

I often think of the astronauts on the last space ad-
venture. How precious of our Lord to have had several
strong, loving Christians on that voyage. Not just one
but several strong people who loved Jesus with all their
hearts and were not ashamed of their precious Lord.

Who is this new creation? This is the one who is created in Christ Jesus. You are so beautiful but have been hidden as though by a veil. Neither the "old you" nor anyone else has seen the real "you" in all her beauty until now. You love the real "you" in Him. You have come to know the real "you" in Him. You are pleasantly surprised as the gifts He placed within you before you were conceived (your spiritual DNA) are now being revealed to you on a regular basis as you worship Him.

What are the gifts He has placed in you to be used by Him and for His purposes? Have you asked Him to show them to you? He will if you ask Him. Let's ask Him. "Precious Lord, please show us these gifts. Thank You. In Jesus' name, Amen."

People will entrust you to share with them what you have experienced for they will see His glory all over your beautiful face because you have been worshipping Him in His secret place!

As you have worshipped Him, you have discovered a deep peace in the center of your "three-part" new "you"—a very restful, special place in Him, a most holy place, and a place of rest—His Sabbath rest.

PART III: HIS ANOINTING

Step 10

Entering Into His Rest

Now we are so intertwined with our Lord and He is with us. Our Lord is holy; therefore He demands us to be also. He keeps us pure and holy (set apart unto Him) by the power of His Holy Spirit living in us and guiding us every step of the way. The sweet Holy Spirit reveals to us more and more each day who our beautiful Jesus really is. The Word comes alive and we are overflowing in His Love. This love, His divine love, manifests in everyday living. Whereas before we might have been very impatient, now we wait, undergirded with His patience. His love flows to our spouse, family, friends, and everyone we meet. We have His wisdom for making wise decisions, therefore saving both time and money. His words flow from our lips as we prayerfully counsel others who may need guidance in their decision-making. We allow Him to love, counsel, and live His Life through us. Though we make plans every day for our future, we also share with Him that He has our permission to interrupt them and do what He chooses to do each day.

When He does, we now do not *react* in frustration because we have learned to flow with His plan.

How beautiful your sandaled feet O prince's daughter (Song of Sol. 7:1a).

Our feet are sandaled because we are active and do not wait for life to happen. No. Life happens as we are in motion: walking, running, swimming, etc. Our feet now go where He directs them, bringing His Good News to everyone we meet. It may be to a neighbor close by, or it may be to a stranger 8,000 miles away from home. Either is fine with us for as we are obedient to Him, He rewards us with more of Himself and there is absolutely nothing else which can compare to being in His sweet tangible presence. This is what causes us to have, *in His eyes, beautiful feet* because He knows they will go wherever He wants them to go.

He rewards us not only for being obedient to Him in important matters, but in little things as well. As we obey Him, we are showing Him we both adore Him and trust Him. He will never disappoint us. He is so precious!

Let this Word impact our lives: "Therefore since the promise of entering into His rest still stands" (Heb. 4a). How glorious that the promise of entering into His rest still stands! Because we have entered into His rest, He now does the work through us.

This is what our Lord is referring to when He says "Let us, therefore, make every effort to enter that rest" (Heb. 4:11). "For anyone who enters God's rest also rests from his own work, just as God did from His" (Heb. 4:10). A *Sabbath rest* is a place *in* Him whereby we no longer minister—touch people *for* Him— but He anoints *Himself* in us and He touches people through us.

His life is lived through each of our one-of-a-kind personality, our own individual uniqueness. He loves variety and the way He shows the people in the world how much He loves them through you is different from the way He does it through someone else. How precious is our Lord Jesus.

What joy it is to have entered into His rest. We are at peace within because we are governed by peace. We are ever vigilant to do what He desires to do each day. Because we have entered into His rest, we begin to walk in the *divine authority of God*.

He heals the sick, raises the dead, and performs all kinds of miracles through us. He is in us and has anointed Himself in us—Christ in us, not us, but *Christ in us* the hope of glory (Col. 1:27). There is such a place of quiet that is deep inside us (deep calls to deep) because we have entered into His rest through His plan, His purpose, and His will. He now lives His life through us.

He has chosen to reveal this awesome mystery to us.

To them God has chosen to make known among the Gentiles the glorious riches of this mystery which is Christ in you the hope of glory (Col. 1:27).

For it isn't us but *Christ in us* that is the awesome revelation. This is His rest. And as long as we *stay* in His rest, we will never experience burnout. For we will follow only His agenda for us each day, not the agenda of someone else for us. Whether we are working in the field of ministry or in the secular field, do not allow other people to place their agendas for you on your shoulders. His destiny for you is glorious and free from burnout.

At this point, He fills us with His precious anointing on a much deeper level for the warfare we will face. And because we have allowed Him to develop His character in us first (the fruit of the Holy Spirit—Gal. 5:22-23), He is now able to manifest His supernatural gifts of the Holy Spirit (1 Cor. 12:8-11) through us at this time for it is no longer we who live but "Christ in you [us] the hope of glory" (Col. 1:27).

When I asked Him a number of years ago about His anointing during the season of total surrender and how to receive Him in greater depth, He said these words to me: "My anointing depends upon your relationship with Me!"

Sweet friend, He has so much for us. His destiny for us is custom-designed. A custom-designed destiny by the Designer of the universe—how awesome is that!

How beautiful He is and how precious we are to Him. No one can worship Him in quite the same way you do. Each one of us is unique; no one else is like us in all His creation!

> *But my dove, my perfect one, is unique, the only daughter of her mother (Song of Sol. 6:9).*

In this level of His rest, He has anointed Himself

within us to do warfare against His enemy. He loves mankind and He is about to take back from the enemy all that he has stolen. He will do it through you. He is the anointed One in you who will raise the dead, open blind eyes, comfort the lonely, and cause the lame to walk. "Christ in you the hope of glory" (Col. 1:27)—not you but Christ in you. The truths He has taught us He will now have us teach to others.

In this season we sense His presence closer to us than ever before, drawing us even closer to Him. We love to have this special time alone with Him.

When we arrive at this point of holding nothing back from Him (even our Isaac), He will bless us in every way possible.

We are strong spiritually because it is no longer we who live but "Christ in you (us) the hope of glory" (Col. 1:27). We are strong mentally because our minds now have the mind of Christ for they have been renewed with the Word of God. We are strong physically because we have saturated ourselves with His Word. By not allowing anger, strife, gossip, etc. to enter into our new selves, therefore, we have given no place to the enemy.

We are blessed with many precious relationships: first, our Lord; and second, family and friends. We are not perfect. The *power* to sin has been broken, but we can still revert to acting in the natural and will occasionally do so as we are being changed from glory to glory for all eternity.

We are generous financially and give greatly to His Gospel because of our love for Him, so we are beginning to reap our financial harvest. He begins to bless us abundantly for all the financial seeds we have sown in famine during our season of total surrender (our precious tears and our cross). They are now coming to fruition in this new season of harvest for the "new you," this "three-part" new creation *in Christ Jesus with a fully transformed spirit, soul, and body* (not yet glorified body but a living sacrifice) now being *changed* from glory to glory. We are *alive in Christ Jesus* and will receive all the "riches stored in secret places" (Is. 15:3b).

He loves us so very, very much. We are precious to Him. He delights to see His face reflected in us.

It is this transformed new creation who is being *changed.* To reiterate, the transformation is a separate and distinct work from *change.* Just as the new birth is separate and distinct from the mighty Baptism of the Holy Spirit, so too is transformation of the old one-part (born again) man separate and distinct from the *change* of the "three-part" new man (new creation).

It is that power, that awesome resurrection power, that is available to us to bind the enemy and all his works; he *is* defeated. We are commanded by the Lord to enforce his defeat! Our Lord has great confidence in us that we will do what He has called us to do. We have placed, in turn, our confidence in the Lord. "I will say of the Lord, He is my refuge and my fortress, my God, in whom I trust" (Ps. 91:2). "For I will hasten my word to perform it" (Jer. 1:12 KJV). We begin to speak forth His Word energized by the sweet Holy Spirit. He watches over His Word for it is filled with power (like dynamite) and He brings His Word to pass. "...and upholding all things by the *word* of *his* Power" (Heb. 1:3a KJV).

How delightful is your love my sister, my bride!
How much more pleasing is your love than wine
and the fragrance of your perfume than any
spice! (Song of Sol. 4:10).

Sweet friend, do you see it? It isn't you but *Christ in*
you the hope of glory! (Col. 1:27) He anoints Himself,
not you, but He anoints Himself *in you* to get the job
done! We must now be alive unto God, not just one part
nor two parts *but all three parts—our spirit, our soul,*
and our body.

"Precious Lord, please reveal this awesome revelation to our new spirit-man. Thank You. We love You. In
Jesus' name, Amen."

His anointing alone sets the captives free. Jesus said
in Luke 4:18-19:

The Spirit of the Lord is on me because he has
anointed me to preach good news to the poor.
He has sent me to proclaim freedom for the pris-
oners and recovery of sight for the blind to re-
lease the oppressed to proclaim the year of the
Lord's favor.

We are beginning to see the wonderful plan of our
heavenly Father. He has shown us our heritage. Because
He is our King and we are His children then we are royalty also.

Step 11

The Royal Overcomer

We now see ourselves as royalty, and as royal children of the Father, we have obligations to fulfill. We are ever on the go fulfilling His assignment, doing what He has asked us to do after having worshipped Him. This is His Kingdom, and we take our places ruling in His Kingdom as His royal children. We have been taught to rule by the sweet Holy Spirit as He rules with justice, mercy, and strength; and we do so also.

Our lips speak with His anointing. His "milk and honey [the sweetness of His Word] are under your tongue" (Song of Sol. 4:11).

We speak life into every situation we encounter. When we are present, the very atmosphere is changed because He is peace and His peace permeates the surroundings. In His Kingdom, we live life to the fullest. When we encounter people who are fearful because of what is taking place around them, we speak His faith and boldly take authority over fear and throw it out. We refuse to live in fear.

It is only those who are free (having gone through the "three-part" total surrender) who can now share with others how they too can be set free. The free are fighters, warriors, well trained by the sweet Holy Spirit and well disciplined, brought about as they read The Song of Solomon. He has changed us into mighty warriors of the King. The future He has for us is awesome!

How has this helped us in our everyday lives? He has made us free in every area. Whatever He has called us to do, we will do. If we can't do it one way, we'll find another way. Because He is counting on us, we would never disappoint Him. Our Father also knows we will complete whatever He has given us to do as His custom-designed assignment. We are His beautiful royal children, no longer hidden under the veil of the cursed Adamic nature and the little foxes, but fully transformed through the Cross having gone through the process of total surrender. We are now fully *in* Christ Jesus and will be sitting with the Father's Son, Jesus, on His throne.

To him who overcomes I will give the right to eat from the tree of life, which is in the paradise of God (Rev. 2:7).

He who overcomes will not be hurt at all by the second death (Rev. 2:11b).

To him who overcomes, I will give some of the

hidden manna. I will also give him a white stone, with a new name written on it, known only to him who receives it (Rev. 2:18b).

To him who overcomes and does my will to the end I will give authority over the nations (Rev. 2:26).

He will rule them with an iron scepter; he will dash them to pieces like pottery—just as I have received authority from my Father (Psalm 2:9; Rev. 2:27).

I will also give him the morning star (Rev. 2:28).

He who overcomes will, like them, be dressed in white. I will never blot out his name from the book of life, but will acknowledge his name before my Father and his angels (Rev. 3:5).

Him who overcomes I will make a pillar in the temple of my God. Never again will he leave it. I will write on him the name of my God and the name of the city of my God, the new Jerusalem which is coming down out of heaven from my God; and I will also write on him my new name (Rev. 3:12).

To Him who overcomes, I will give the right to

sit with me on my throne, just as I overcame and sat down with my Father on his throne (Rev. 3:21).

We are ruling with Him over His Kingdom of righteousness, peace and joy in the Holy Spirit. We are mighty children of the King, who speak His words with His authority, oversee the administrative tasks of ruling, and make wise decisions after having talked things over with Him.

When people see us they stand back, for we are clothed in His glory. We are not intimidated—neither by man nor by demons. We are secure in our position as His children so the position another holds is immaterial to us. We know there is no position higher than that of being a member of His royal family. We are majestic with His majesty covering us. We are highly favored children of the King. His favor goes before us; whatever door He chooses to open for us will open in due time.

They overcame him by the blood of the Lamb and by the word of their testimony (Rev. 12:11).

Sweet children of the King, He wants us to run after Him. He is so precious. And as we run after Him He will turn around and sweep us up into His arms as a daddy does with his precious little child. We run after Him now with joy, laughter, and child-like abandon that is unlike anything else. We are royal children of our Father, deeply loved and cherished because we are in His Son Jesus ("Christ in me [us] the hope of glory" (Col. 1:27).

We come into that special place where no demon can

go and are carried on the wings of adoration into His heavenly throne room.

> *Yet a time is coming and has now come when the true worshippers will worship the Father in spirit and in truth, for they are the kind of worshippers the Father seeks (John 4:23).*

There may be many who minister *for* our heavenly Father but we have found the secret to His Heart. We minister *to* our heavenly Father by bringing Him pleasure by worshipping Him through The Song of Solomon. We have become intimate worshippers without equal and have the countenance of an intimate worshipper wherever we go because it is He who shines in His glory through us.

As He sees His beauty in us, how does that make Him feel? He feels loved knowing we went through the pain of the Cross for one purpose only and that was to have *all* of Him. He knows we love Him to that depth, even though we have not yet seen Him with our natural eyes. He now knows the depth of our love for Him.

If we go through total surrender and are transformed 100%, then there is no area of our lives that Satan can use to bring about our downfall. If we leave one minute area of the natural man not dealt with, Satan will at some point use it to bring about our destruction—especially if we are in an influential position and use this position to bring glory to our heavenly Father. This is why it is so key to go through total surrender, including the final sacrifice, and not leave even one small place through which the enemy can penetrate.

It is also important to guard this new life (as one guards a baby)—through...
Worship
By reading The Song of Solomon
Out loud
To Him
Every day
In His secret place
With no distractions.

We can't afford to be lazy. "The enemy goes about as a roaring lion seeking whom he may devour." He cannot devour us nor our family *if* we stand against him.

We have to allow our Lord to keep us safe every day as we do our part and continue to grow in our knowledge and in intimacy with Him.

We are people of excellence. From now until Jesus comes for His Bride, we have to continue to put Him first. He is so precious.

We are now in the process of being changed into His image and likeness and will continue to grow and expand into more of His beauty and loveliness, beginning now and throughout eternity!

Please don't ever place anyone or anything else before Him. He loves us and nobody can worship Him in quite the same way you do. You are precious to Him!

We must be on our guard against the wiles of the enemy. This isn't a case whereby we can now relax. No! Although the enemy now has no place in us through transformation, we can lose this wonderful intimacy with our Lord if we choose to become lazy and quit being intimate with Him. Remember He said, "Read out loud The Song of Solomon *every day*!" I believe He means He wants intimacy with His Bride every day!

If we do miss our secret time with Him, we should not let the enemy place us under any condemnation, but rather sincerely repent to our Lord. We should ask His forgiveness for not having put Him *first* and tell Him how much we love Him and truly adore Him and how much living with Him in His secret place means to us. Don't make excuses—the "this", "that", and the "other" of daily living were accomplished that day, but He was left without our precious worship. He is there, waiting for us! He loves us! Let's never say, "Well, I blew it, forget it, it's over." No! It is *not* over. We can sincerely repent and *get up and go* once again into His secret place reserved only for our precious Bridegroom and *us*, His beloved Bride.

Our sweet, heavenly Father loves us and has chosen us to be the Bride for His Son Jesus. How awesome is that! He knew there would come a day when we would fall madly and passionately in love with His beautiful Son, Jesus. We are precious to Him because Jesus said:

I in them and you in me. May they be brought to complete unity to let the world know that you sent me and have loved them even as you have loved me (John 17:23).

We are no longer living in the nature of the first Adam. We are now living in the divine nature of the Last Adam, Christ Jesus. All He has He shares with us. "Now if we are children, then we are heirs, heirs of God and co-heirs with Christ" (Rom. 8:17a).

Step 12

The Royal Children Ruling and Reigning

As we, His beautiful new creation in Christ Jesus go forth, we begin to discover just who we really are.

We have become our heavenly Father's treasured royal children in the image and beauty of His only begotten Son, Jesus, the first born from the dead (1 Cor. 15:45).

For as in Adam all die, so in Christ all will be made alive (1 Cor. 15:22).

So it is written: The first man, Adam, became a living being. The last Adam, a life giving spirit (1 Cor. 15:45).

The first man was of the dust of the earth, the second man from heaven (1 Cor. 15:47).

And just as we have borne the likeness of the earthly man, so shall we bear the likeness of the man from heaven (1 Cor. 15:49).

Because of the Last Adam (Jesus) and what He has done on the Cross, this scripture is now applicable for His transformed Bride now in the process of being changed into His image and likeness.

All beautiful you are, my darling, there is no flaw in you (Song of Sol. 4:7).

That whole creation was destroyed by the Cross and the Blood of Jesus. Jesus is the Last Adam. So we, who are now the transformed children of our heavenly Father, can partake of His position as the Last Adam and become His new creation. Little by little as we grow and expand, that truth will sink in; and when it does, we will be amazed at who we are in Christ. This mystery hidden throughout the ages is revealed to us, the end-time people of this age. We will continue to grow and expand for all eternity—a new creation, His mirror image. When He looks into our faces He should see Himself, His beauty, His kindness, His love, His gentleness, His forgiveness, and all of His other wonderful attributes.

As we continue to operate as His ambassadors, He will continue to reveal truth to us. "Sanctify them by the truth; your word is truth" (John 17:17).

The more we continue to worship Him, the more He will continue to reveal His Word to us. Jesus is the Word, and no matter how much we know, there will always be more depth of Him for us to come to know for all eternity.

Jesus is the Last Adam, fully God and fully Man. He lived as an anointed Son of God is called to live. He is our example. Once we are transformed, Satan (sin) has no more power over us. We have and will always have our own free will. We can choose to react in the natural (Satan wins) or we can choose to respond in the Spirit (then we win and Satan loses). Though we can and may at times react instead of respond, the *power* of sin is broken. That old "you" is gone—blown to smithereens on the Cross—annihilated, out of existence, no longer existing on the planet nor anywhere else.

We will *feel* different and will continue to do so as the days, weeks, months, and years go on forever. This new creation is the same one who will see Him in heaven because we are not in the first Adam, but we are now the "three-part" new you in Christ Jesus, the last Adam. "Christ in you the hope of glory" (Col. 1:27). Just as He is, we are now on this earth being *changed* into the beauty and loveliness of His Son Jesus, beginning now and throughout eternity.

Jesus is the Last Adam, the anointed Son of God. Jesus laid aside His divinity for a season when He agreed with His Father and the sweet Holy Spirit to become man for all eternity—fully God and fully man. No one Person from the Godhead (the Trinity—Father, Son and Holy Spirit) had ever taken on man's being. But Jesus said He would do it in order to save man from Satan and his works of darkness. When Jesus was here on earth, He lived as any other human from childhood through to adulthood. It was only after He had been baptized by John and the Holy Spirit came upon Him that He then had the power to defeat Satan for us.

Come! He eagerly waits to hear our sweet voices telling Him how much we adore Him!
Lover speaking:

You who dwell in the gardens with friends in attendance, Let me hear your voice (Song of Sol. 8:13).

We choose to walk close to Him since we have discovered by falling in love with Him how kind, just, and loving He truly is. He longs for us even more than we hunger and thirst for Him. He chose us for Himself! Glory! We are so precious to Him, and nobody else can take our place!

It is those of us who are alive in this generation who truly understand intimacy with our Lord (though there were others in other generations, but they were few and far between and grossly misunderstood by their contemporaries). We hunger for Him and will not take "No" for an answer. Nobody can stop us. We are His transformed army. There has never been a generation like us before, and there will never be a generation like us in the future (Joel 2:2). For it is not us but "Christ in you [us] the hope of glory" (Col. 1:27). The third day Christian is His three-part new creation Bride. Glory!

The Song of Solomon is for us, the Bride of Christ. He is revealing The Song of Solomon to us as He has never done before to any other generation. Why? Because the sweet Holy Spirit is preparing the Bride for her Bridegroom and teaching us every day how our beautiful Bridegroom wants to be loved by us as we:

Worship
By reading The Song of Solomon
Out loud
To Him
Every day
In His secret place
With no distractions.

We live to bring joy to Him each and every day. That which He has done in us will soon be reflected through us. Come and let us worship our King, Jesus, the Last Adam.

PART V: HIS TRANSFORMED BRIDE

Step 13

Outward Signs of Inward Transformation

The Bride is the Father's gift to His Son. He has chosen a Bride for His only begotten first-born Son of the new creation. He has promised Him a Bride who will be just like Him in Spirit: kind, gentle, passionate, strong, loving, full of joy, full of His glory, with the same heart and the same desires.

What He loves, she will love. What He abhors, she too will abhor and stay far away from. She lives to bring pleasure to Him and joy to His sweet heart and to kiss His beautiful face. She loves her Bridegroom and will do whatever He asks her. For she knows He is pure, holy, and trustworthy. She has a quiet inward peace deep in her spirit because she trusts fully in Him.

Our heart's desire is to do the will of our Lord to fulfill His destiny for us. We are filled with His love for others and we spend time daily in His secret place worshipping Him. We are people of wisdom for our minds are constantly being renewed with the Word of God. As a tree plants its roots firmly into the soil, so too we plant ours firmly into His Word. His Word causes us to live in victory.

This Word, His Living Word, we impart to others as He directs on a regular basis. Our hearts delight to see the fruit which has developed in their lives as a result of His Word now firmly established in them. Our gentleness (which really is not ours but His) we readily give to others for we can see in their eyes how weighed down they are with the worries and cares of this world. We smile His life-affirming smile; we hug with His anointed hug. We make every day count and deposit something good into each one we meet, something of Him—His love, kindness, concern, and smile. People can sense that it is really God in us who is ministering life to them when we tell them how much Jesus loves them.

We bless our employers with His wisdom flowing from us in answer to perplexing problems no one was able to solve. They see His steadfastness in us as we are known as those who will stay with the project and see it through to its completion. He is truth; therefore, we speak His truth. We do not compromise yet cover our words of correction to another with His love and grace.

We are like the fragrance of spring (He is the Rose of Sharon) and bubble forth with His joy in situations where there is no joy. We are His messenger and He knows He can count on us, for we listen and obey His precious voice.

Our spirit-man has made room for Him as we have

allowed all the old to die to make room for the new creation in Christ Jesus (Col. 1:27).

After a while we begin to *feel* different on the inside. We may look the same on the outside, but we *know* we are totally different on the inside (long before His glory shines through us from the inside to the outside). We don't say anything to anyone, but they'll see it for themselves when what He has done *in* us will be reflected *through* us.

If we want His precious signature fragrance, His perfume of love, emanating through us we need to stay "up close and personal" with our heavenly Bridegroom. We need to let Him know, always, how precious He is to us.

I held him and would not let him go (Song of Sol. 3:4a).

He'll always be so gentle and loving. He loves us and wants to impart His fragrance of love, joy, peace, patience, etc. to us on a daily basis.

The "three-part" new creation Bride is the most beautiful of all the works of His hand. It is this Bride whom everyone longs to see. She is being unveiled more in these Last Days than ever before because after all the generations of man from Adam until now He has finally found a generation who will pay the supreme sacrifice (transformation) so she can have all of Him. She has tasted and found Him to be irresistible. She will do whatever she must in order to have Him. This causes His heart to leap with joy to know He is so loved by the creation for whom He died.

Beautiful Bride, wife of the Lamb, you are filled with His élan, His love, His spice, and His truth too. He died to reveal the new you. In the days ahead, He is planning to reveal more and more of you, His special new creation Bride.

Step 14

Sons of God Revealed Through His New Creation Bride

We are the generation that is to be revealed to all creation. It is through us that His glorious plan for the ages is being revealed—Christ in you, "the hope of glory" (Col. 1:27).

Just as Jesus' lifestyle is obedience to His Father, our lifestyle now becomes obedience to our Lord. Where He leads, we will follow.

His Bride is the new Jerusalem!

Come I will show you the bride, the wife of The Lamb (Rev. 21:9b).

And he carried me away in the Spirit to a mountain great and high and showed me the Holy City, Jerusalem, coming down out of heaven from God. It shone with the glory of God and its brilliance was like that of a very pre-

cious jewel, like a jasper, clear as crystal (Rev. 21:9a-11).

It is this Bride, His "three-part" new creation Bride, whom He is revealing to the world just before He comes to take her to Himself (in the Rapture) to the Marriage Supper of the Lamb. "The Spirit and the bride say 'Come!'" (Rev. 22:17).

A glorious future awaits us! It is this new creation Bride, who now lives in His Holy of Holies, who will live there forever throughout all eternity. It is this Bride, a mirror image of her precious Bridegroom, who is madly, wildly, passionately in love with Him and wants the whole world to know Him as she does!

Who are these new creation sons/daughters of God? They are the overcomers in Christ Jesus.

"My Bride, My beautiful transformed Bride, so like Myself. I love you. For she loves Me and has proven her love by the Cross. The Cross is the benchmark, the plumb-line I use. ("God will stretch out over Eden the measuring line of chaos and the plumb-line of desolation" [Is. 34:11]). It is the Cross that I myself had to endure for you and so will you *if* you want All Me. *If* you want to know Me intimately. *If* you want Me to empower you to use you in depths of My Anointing you have not yet experienced. I am looking for totally surrendered vessels—not "name" vessels but surrendered vessels. If you will allow Me to put you through the Cross, the whole Cross, then you too will know Me as your intimate holy Bridegroom. I reward those who obey Me. They are those who know Me intimately. You can see it on their faces; love cannot be hidden.

There are many who pretend to know Me but do not. They may fool some but they cannot fool the true intimate worshippers. For their faces are like Moses' face. No shame. All glory—My glory—reflected through them.

My intimate worshippers and I share secrets which are only given in My Holy of Holies.

My Bride obeys Me—even when it is hard to do so in the natural realm. Because she obeys Me, I can use her to bless many others; you never bless another that I in turn do not bless you. You see many who are blessed in My Church. It isn't because I love them more, it is because they are more obedient and thus I can use them for My glory in more situations."

There are several billion people all around the world who desperately want Him but don't know how to find Him. He will use us, His new creation Bride to reach the ones who are searching. In these Last Days, He will not use the counterfeit Christian but the real blood bought precious Bride. And the world will finally see the difference between the one who is madly in love with her Bridegroom and the one who *says* she is but her lifestyle speaks volumes to the contrary.

Sweet Bride, He is drawing forth His Bride to Himself from all languages, tribes, peoples, and nations. He loves us!

Nobody else can take our place. Nobody! He's waiting for us. He loves us., and soon all members of His Bride will reflect the beauty and loveliness of our Holy, compassionate, kind and passionate, precious Bridegroom, our Lord Jesus!

"My Bride takes pleasure in knowing Me, Her Bridegroom, in intimacy. She has allowed herself to become totally vulnerable to Me—to My Plans and Purposes for her destiny.

My Bride is the one I love. She is the one who came forth from within Me, just as Eve came forth from within Adam.

My Bride is beautiful because she is indwelt by My beauty, My holiness, My passionate love, My compassion, My joy, My peace, My righteousness.

My Bride fills Me with joy. My joy expressed through her own personality offered with her love up to Me."

She is like no other. She is His queen; He is her King.

His peace and gentleness have now become a part of her new nature. We are priceless to Him because we have chosen Him for all eternity. He is priceless to us because He has redeemed us.

Jesus loves us, sweet Bride, so very, very much. He loves all members of His Bride and is asking all of us to go through total surrender. In this way, He can have the deepest intimacy with all His Bride. He desires transformation with all His Bride—all those He is calling to the Marriage Supper of the Lamb. Why? Because He sees in us Himself, His beauty, His kindness, His gentleness, and His anointing, and she has been trained by the sweet Holy Spirit how to bring pleasure to her Holy Bridegroom. To the degree we *know* Him intimately, is to the degree we can have His presence and His anointing resting in and upon us.

The sweet Holy Spirit is wooing several billion of us around the world to go through the process of total surrender so we can emerge on Resurrection Day a Bride without flaw. When He comes in His glory, He will manifest it through His new creation Bride. His glory is His presence of love, strength, kindness, joy, peace, patience, and gentleness—His essence now *transferred* into our being.

Because we are now one spirit with our precious Bridegroom, His glory shines forth through us in all His brilliance. Does this mean we are perfect? Only He is perfect. Because we are now in Him fully and completely as His new creation Bride, we are perfect *but only in Him.*

But my dove, my perfect one is unique (Song of Sol. 6:9a).

Our spirit-man who is in Him is perfect. We, however, still live in a physical body and can at any time choose to exercise our own free will and react in the flesh (though the *power* of sin is broken your free will is still yours).

The heavenly host and all creation rejoice to see His awesome plan hidden throughout the ages and revealed in this generation through us, His new creation Bride. How do we differ from anyone else? We have His divine passionate nature living (dwelling) in us. We have His authority to deal with situations, and His anointing to set the captives free. Before we, as His Bride, can preach or teach anything, He will make sure we have been in similar situations and have emerged as overcomers. He will then have us live in them for a while before He will set us free (like a race horse) to go and teach others what He has taught us.

Beautiful Bride, we are glorious with His glory shining upon us and through us. We are the sons and daughters of God being revealed to all creation. His beautiful Bride shining like the sun (transformed) and changed *with His glory* never before seen until now. We are precious to Him!

He is calling several billion men and women around the world to become born again! He loves mankind and is so eager to come back for us!

Our beautiful born-again spirit is no longer hidden beneath the veil of flesh (Adam's fallen nature) but is now emerging into the full light of day for all creation to see as we eagerly await the soon coming of our Holy beautiful Bridegroom, our precious Lord Jesus.

Sweet Bride, we are almost there!

Who is this that appears like the dawn, fair as the moon, bright as the sun, majestic as the stars in procession? (Song of Sol. 6:10).

We are now clothed with Him, with His glory—this exceptional, supernatural, passionate love.

Step 15

Exceptional Love

Oh, sweet Bride, what word picture do you see when you read the words: exceptional and love?

A number of years ago, the Lord had begun to heal our marriage after we had received Jesus as our Lord and Saviour through the altar call at a Billy Graham Evangelistic Association© movie. This movie had been shown at a neighborhood theater near our home in Honolulu, Hawaii. Shortly thereafter, our Lord led us to the first Marriage Encounter© weekend ever held in Hawaii, where He continued and completed His healing process.

At this time, my husband and I arrived home after having spent the weekend with other couples at the Marriage Encounter, said goodnight to our babysitter, and kissed each one of our four small sleeping children good-night. We then went downstairs to our master bedroom, knelt down by our king-size bed, held hands, and prayed the following prayer: "Lord Jesus, we thank you so much for healing our marriage. Please show us each day how to love (Joey) (Helen) with your love the way (Joey) (Helen) want to be loved. Now Lord, please give us the kind of marriage Adam and Eve had *before* the Fall! In Jesus' name, Amen."

Wow! Did He ever answer that prayer! A few months later, I had a face-to-face encounter with our Lord. He took out all the hurts, sadness, and grief (our baby twin son had also died as well as our marriage). In exchange He gave me His love and said, "I have now filled you with My love, My supernatural, passionate love. Now go and love your husband with My supernatural love. He is My *gift* to you!" (My husband also had had an encounter with Him shortly before and He gave him His supernatural, passionate love for me!) Our Lord is so good.

Every day He showed us how the other wanted to be loved. Every day He showed us how to build each other up and not tear each other down. Every day He showed us how important little things are, i.e., flowers for me; listening with *my* full attention to my husband; date night every week (get a sitter; even if you are tired, get dressed up and go) but don't talk about kids, finances, etc., instead rekindle the romance you had when you were dating and you only had eyes for each other. Listen to hurt feelings (feelings are valid); feel the other person's pain, then healing (and kisses!) can take place; talk and listen to each other; put Jesus first, sweetheart/spouse second, then kids, etc.; dance with each other at home as well as out; always keep the fire burning after the kids are in bed!

In the end when the kids are grown and gone, you

will only have each other and if you sow passionate seeds of love now those years will be full of passion and romance. We did; He did; and they were!

It was so devastating when the one I adored died because he had loved me for 15 out of 27 years of marriage with the supernatural, passionate love of Jesus.

This is also why it was very easy for me to respond to our Lord when He said, "I'll be your Lover!" How Lord? "Through The Song of Solomon."

That is why we all need His supernatural love with which to love our spouse, kids, friends, colleagues, etc. He *loves* them through us!

Let Him show you how to love your spouse with His love. If you treat him (your spouse) as your king, then soon he will treat you as his queen and vice versa.

This is the kind of exceptional passionate, supernatural love He wants your marriage to have as well. He'll do it for you; all you have to do is ask! He loves you so!

(If your marriage has serious problems, seek the Lord and ask Him to lead you to the best marriage counselor.) Just as my husband and I loved to dance with each other, our Lord loves it when we dance before Him. He is so precious.

Step 16

Within the Veil

Sweet Bride, He has opened His doors wide for both men and women to become His Bride. Of course, women relate differently to the Lord from the way men do. Both ways (men's and women's) are delightful to His heart. Oh sweet Bride! He loves us! He is calling out to us! Let's stop and worship Him now. He is so worthy.

"Precious Lord Jesus, we, your "three-part" (transformed) new creation Bride, adore you and are passionately in love with You. Please draw us ever closer to the place of intimacy in Your heart. Thank You, sweetest Jesus, our Lord. In Jesus' name, Amen."

Because we have been totally transformed, He has now filled us with Himself. He is Passion. His Passion is a Person (not a thing nor a force). His Name? His Name is the sweet Holy Spirit. He is so precious, and He is the One who is revealing to us who our beautiful handsome Bridegroom really is. All this time He has loved us with His divine, passionate love through the Person of the sweet Holy Spirit. We, in turn, for the most part have loved Him with our human love. This was before transformation because even though we were born again and spirit-filled, we were filled with so much of the old Adamic nature (hatred, anger, jealousy, and gossip). He had very little room in us for His love because of the old "you" and "me," the little foxes and self.

But now, ah! This generation is different. He has poured out upon us His Holy Spirit, who has been wooing us to the heart of our Bridegroom. For so many generations He has held back His passionate love as our Bridegroom for His Bride. But this generation—all of us are coming to know Him like this—are His Passionate Bride, madly in love with Him.

Why? Because the sweet Holy Spirit is preparing us, His beautiful Bride, to get ready for His soon return. He loves us and eagerly longs for us to be with Him.

Oh sweet friend, what a future awaits us! It is glorious!

Now that we reflect Him in *all* His Glory, He now reveals us to the world. They are astounded when they see us for they knew us before transformation. But now we are bright as the sun (His Light) and walk with royal bearing no matter where we go or what we do. It is not important to us to be number one. We want Him to be number one.

Our faces are radiant with His glory and His presence. We have no shame because we have been totally set free through His transforming work in us. We are set free to love, laugh, dance, sing, and let the child within come forth and play.

We have found our Song of Solomon! He is coming

back for His Bride who loves Him very deeply and passionately. This precious book from the Old Testament has shown us how to have the deepest face-to-face encounter with our Lord. He loves us and He is delighted to have become our very own Song of Solomon. We are His beautiful, passionate Bride without spot or wrinkle in Him!

The Spirit and the bride say "Come!" (Rev. 22:17).

Oh what a precious friend our Lord has become to us. In fact, has He not become our very best friend? And now He is giving us the privilege to enter within the veil and to become His very own beautiful blood-bought Bride. He died for us because He loves us. He died for His Bride. He loves her so. He wanted a Bride who would passionately love Him as a bride on earth who is deeply in love with her bridegroom loves Him. He is passionately in love with His Bride and wants her to know this.

And each and every member of His Bride is so special to Him. No one else could ever take your place. He planned for us to be His Bride even before we were conceived. This revelation is so awesome that when it hits you, you won't be able to sleep because you will be so awestruck at the magnificent plan of our heavenly Father. "Whosoever will may come." He has no cliques, no favorites. All of us who receive and love His only begotten Son, Jesus, become His candidates to become the Bride for His Son. It is the new creation Bride who is in Christ.

...far above all rule and authority, power and dominion and every title that can be given not only in the present age but also in the one to come (Ephesians 1:21).

Taste and see that the Lord is good (Psalm 34:8a).

When we have tasted His sweetness, we become addicted to Him. Every day we want more and more of Him. Just call to Him! Tell Him out loud how much your heart longs for Him. He loves to hear our sweet voices calling to Him. As we call to Him, He will answer us. "Jesus, sweet Lord, we love You, precious Lord!"

Just imagine if we had not taken the time to have fallen in love with Him by *worshipping Him through reading The Song of Solomon.* Could we really, really ever have known how beautiful He says we are, how lovely we are to Him(Song of Sol. 6:4a), and how proud He is of us? (Song of Sol. 6:9)

Oh, how He loves us. He has given us the most beautiful, romantic, passionate book of the Bible through which we can fall in love with Him! (Song of Sol. 6:3)

Now that we have been transformed and are in the process of being changed into His beauty and loveliness, we see what an awesome work the Lord has done for us. This in itself has caused us to fall even more in love with Him.

Our Lord loves us so much. He is our precious Bridegroom and loves us as His beloved Bride. How does a bridegroom love his bride? With passion, romance, gentleness, and kindness. He protects her and tells her how much he loves her. He tells her that she is the one he chose above all others. He tells her how beautiful she is and how lovely her mouth is. He speaks gently to her. He is very proud of her and wants everybody to know that this beautiful lady who is leaning on his arm belongs to him.

Our Lord feels the same way about us.

How beautiful you are, my darling! Oh how beautiful. Your eyes are doves (Song of Sol. 1:15).

He protects us.

He has taken me to the banquet hall and his banner over me is love (Song of Sol. 2:4).

He is so proud of us.

But my dove, my perfect one, is unique, the only daughter of her mother (Song of Sol. 6:9a).

He embraces us.

His left arm is under my head and his right arm embraces me (Song of Sol. 2:6).

You will feel His tangible presence and His presence is like none other.

This is my lover, this my friend O daughters of Jerusalem (Song of Sol. 5:16).

Now the love talk between our Lord and us is so loving and comes as easily as breathing. We call Him by special names which touch His heart (like "precious" and "beautiful one").

My lover is radiant and ruddy outstanding among 10,000 (Song of Sol. 5:10).

We now want the whole world to know how precious He is. He uses us to bring about His love to others as His love flows through us now unhindered by the old Adamic nature that was forever annihilated!

Who is this coming up from the desert leaning on her lover (Song of Sol. 8:5).

This scripture is so real now to us because we have been leaning on our Lord—totally dependent on Him. Gone is the independent "I'll do it my way" spirit, and in its place is the "Lord, please show me Your way" spirit. We have no desires but His, no dreams but His, no plans but His. We only live through Him. We want what He wants and love what He loves because we are His. The season of total surrender, including our final sacrifice, accomplished this in our lives.

He loves us so and no one, absolutely no one else, can take our place in His eyes. "Sweet Lord, You are so precious. Please draw us ever closer to You. We love you."

As we stand in His presence, we are standing on Holy Ground in His divine glory, His very essence. As we come to see Him in His glory, we are awed by His loveliness, His beauty, and His majesty. His glory is like nothing else. It is as we come into His presence through The Song of Solomon that we have a taste of His glory.

What is His glory? It is His very presence. It is this presence that is going to cover the earth as the waters cover the sea in these Last Days.

For the earth will be full of the knowledge of the Lord as the waters cover the sea (Is. 11:9).

How will He cover the earth with His glory? Through us, His beautiful transformed, new creation Bride. Because we have fallen in love with Him, it is His Light shining now through us. It is this Light that draws all men unto Himself. It is He who reveals Himself in all His beauty (His glory) to the world through His beautiful Bride. It is she who passionately tells others how glorious her Lord is, and they see His beauty reflected in her. His beauty cannot be bought no matter how much we offer. No! This kind of beauty only comes as a direct result of having gone through the Cross. He keeps this beauty in reserve for those who are *dead* to the old Adamic nature and alive to the new—the "three-part" new creation in Christ Jesus.

Oh, sweet Bride, because we are passionately in love with Him we shine like the sun.

Who is this that appears like the dawn, fair as the moon, bright as the sun (Song of Sol. 6:10a).

It shows in our eyes, our face, our walk, our talk, and our lifestyle, which is now wholly devoted to Him. He longs to draw others into this intimacy He has been so gracious to have shared with us. He is so precious! He is no respecter of persons and His heart's cry is for His beloved new creation Bride. For when He sees her, He sees Himself in her because she is now a partaker of His divine nature!

When His glory comes as we worship, we stand still as we behold His beauty and savor every moment of His loving embrace. His holy supernatural love will begin to envelop you as the bridal veil discreetly covers the bride. This is His reward for those who have gone through the Cross (final sacrifice) and have now come forth as pure gold, gold that shimmers in the sunlight without flaw.

> *But he knows the way that I take. When he has tested me, I will come forth as gold" [transformed and now being "changed" into His image and likeness] (Job 23:10).*

Can you imagine how beautiful it will be when all His Bride has been transformed? He is coming for all members of His Bride, and His heart's desire is for her to be ready for His soon return.

"Precious Lord, we thank you so much for transforming us. We Your Bride are passionately in love with You! We love You so much! Come, Precious Lord, please, we adore You."

Our Lord loves it when we dance before Him. The dance is part of our worship and in these Last Days many of His intimate worshippers who are within His Bride are dancing before Him a beautiful worship dance—soft and flowing and full of adoration for our King. He loves it. If you have not done it, try it and as tears course down your cheeks, you will know that once again, you, His Bride, have brought pleasure to His sweet heart. Look for ways to bring pleasure to Him. He is so precious and loves us so very much.

And as we dance before Him, He will share a secret with us. What is that secret? I can't tell you, but I'll give you a hint. You may start out dancing alone, but you won't end up dancing alone. He'll reveal this secret to you as you dance before Him, and when He does, you will crumble to the floor after the last dance because of the significance of this precious revelation of love shared only with His Bride in His Holy of Holies because she has taken the time to dance with her Bridegroom alone. "Precious Lord, we adore you so!"

His Heart overflows with love for His Bride. He wants her to have His very best since she has given Him her very best (the Cross). Just as it was excruciatingly painful for Him to go through the Cross, He knows how hard it was for His Bride as well.

This love, His tangible presence, He gives to His passionate Bride in His secret chambers, His Holy of Holies. He who is the very essence of love lives in us. Because we have been transformed He now has taken up residence in us. There is nothing in us which is displeasing to Him and He now comes to *abide*—live in us—not just to visit but to live in and dwell in us on a permanent basis. He transfers His Holy of Holies into us for all eternity.

Does that mean that however much we know Him

now that for all eternity we stop there? No. What it does mean is this: our oneness will never change but our depth or degree of oneness will.

We become one Spirit with Him, and from that moment on we grow in depth of passion for our Bridegroom from now and throughout eternity.

Soon there will be the Call of the Trumpet to come to the Marriage Supper of the Lamb.

Do you know anyone who has ever attended a royal banquet in heaven? The reception for our Bridegroom and His Bride? It is as if our Father were issuing the following wedding invitation to All Creation:

The Heavenly Father
requests the joy of your presence at
The Marriage Supper of the Lamb
and His Beautiful Bride
which will take place in heaven in the near future.
Please respond immediately.

Just as a wedding planner oversees every last detail of the wedding, our heavenly Father is overseeing every last detail of the wedding between His Son and His beautiful Bride.

Just think—we are His beautiful Bride, hand-picked (chosen) by our Father for His only begotten Son, Jesus.

Soon that glorious wedding day will be upon us. The host of heaven will look on with delight as our heavenly Father takes the hand of His Son and the hand of His Bride and unites them together in Holy Matrimony for all eternity. The sound of the harp is heard, the violins too, as our Bridegroom will tenderly hold you as you dance together The Lover's Dance—the dance He chose just for you.

Sweet, sweet Bride! If for any reason you are not able to dance physically before our Lord, I have great news for you! A number of years ago before I left my beautiful Hawaii, I was driving my convertible Mustang with the top down. I had a beautiful worship tape in the cassette player, and I was worshipping with my voice out loud as I drove. When I came to a stoplight while waiting for the light to turn green, I raised my hands in worship to our King and just allowed them to flow in poetic motions to the timing of the music. In Hawaii, the beautiful Christian Hula dance is everywhere and as you dance, your graceful hula hands play a large part in expressing the story in poetic motion. This day as I was worshipping with my hands, a young teenager stopped for the light in the traffic lane beside me. When he asked me what I was doing, I smiled at him and told him I was worshipping our Lord. Because he was from Hawaii and had grown up with the beautiful hula dance, he said, "Oh, I get it—you are dancing with your hands!" "Yes, that was exactly it!" I said smiling. I was dancing with my hands while still sitting behind the wheel of the car waiting for the light to change.

And so, sweet friend, if you cannot physically jump up and down or dance, the sweet Holy Spirit will show you how to dance with your hands before Our Lord! He is so precious! He does not want you to miss out on the beautiful worship dance. He will teach you His very special dance just for you.

Dance, sweet Bride! He loves you! You are so precious to Him! He is your priceless Pearl.

Step 17

Jesus—The Priceless Pearl

A pearl is beautiful yet strong. It shines in its luminescence! As we come into His Presence through worship, we partake of His light and His beauty. As we bask in His glow, when we leave His holy chambers and return to doing the everyday things of life, we leave with something of Him on us—His transcendent light of holiness. For He is our Holy Lord. When Moses came down from the mountain, his face shone with the glory of God. He had been in His Presence.

> *When Moses came down from Mount Sinai with the two tablets of the Testimony in his hands, he was not aware that his face was radiant because he had spoken with the Lord (Ex. 34:29).*

Jesus is the priceless Pearl. He paid the highest price to redeem us! He paid with His life. He paid with His Blood. There is no price we could put on what Jesus did for us. They tried to when He was sold for 30 pieces of

107

silver. How can you put a price on what is priceless?

Jesus is unique. Have you ever known anyone else who could die for your sins or open the seven seals? No, and you never will. He is without equal. The light of the knowledge of the Glory of God is in the *face of Jesus Christ* (2 Cor. 4:6b), the sinless Son of God.

In the priceless Pearl, all the fullness of deity dwells in bodily form—all His power and all His authority over the enemy, death, sickness, disease, despair, poverty, *fear*, and all things which are under the law of sin and death.

In the priceless Pearl resides:
- All holiness
- All joy
- All peace
- All righteousness
- All kindness
- All forgiveness
- All resurrection power.

Jesus is the man, fully God and fully man, and He is Jesus the Christ—the Anointed One. He is empowered by the Holy Spirit. Jesus was conceived by the Holy Ghost but had no power until the Holy Ghost came upon Him. Though He is God, He laid aside His divinity and lived on this earth as a man anointed by the Holy Spirit.

For in Christ all the fullness of the Deity lives in bodily form (Col. 2:9).

All the fullness—His wisdom, knowledge, under-standing, kindness, gentleness, and truthfulness lives in us because *we are in Christ.* "Christ in you the hope of glory" (Col. 1:27).

Who is His Resurrection Power?

• He is none other than a Person
• The anointing of the Holy Spirit
• He is a Person—not an it, not a force.
• He is the Third Person of the Holy Trinity.
• He is the One who raised Jesus from the dead.
• He is the One who lives inside you when you
    become born-again.
• He is the Comforter.
• He is Love.
• He is Peace.
• He is Joy.

Jesus is seated at the right hand of the Father in His glorified body. The Holy Spirit comes to live within us when we ask Jesus to come into our heart (Romans 8:9 and 10). And He comes *upon* (up and on) us when we ask for the mighty Baptism of the Holy Spirit (Acts 2:4).

Who (*not what*) is Resurrection Power? Resurrection Power is a *Person*—the sweet, precious Holy Spirit! He is available to us. *All power* is in a *Person*, not a thing. Dynamite power is *encased* in an *object*, i.e., a *stick* of dynamite. *God's power* is *encapsulated* in a *Person*.

And if the Spirit of him who raised Jesus from the dead is living in you, he who raised Christ from the dead will also give life to your mortal bodies through his Spirit, who lives in you (Romans 8:11).

The Person of the Holy Spirit encloses all divine power. Resurrection Power is:
- A Person.
- The *Person* of the Holy Spirit.
- He is divine ability.
- He is divine anointing.
- He is *power*!

All power resides, rests, dwells, and lives in Him. He now is available to live in us in His anointing. It takes power, the dynamic power who is God, the Third Person of the Holy Trinity. He is the power, the explosion who raised Jesus from the dead. He who is power Himself lives in us. This dynamic power Person, the Holy Spirit, is available to us in these Last Days. This is the One who is on the other side of the Cross. He is the One whom Paul experienced. He is the One whom all the apostles experienced when they
- Healed the sick
- Cast out demons
- Raised the dead.

It was not they but Christ *The Anointed One of God* in them the hope of glory (Col. 1:27) who performed these miracles. This is why we need to surrender to His will and go through the Cross, for it is only as we are *dead* to the old nature and all its effects of sin that He the Anointing of God can come and have full rein in us.

He anoints Himself to do the work, not us but Christ *in us*! If we have surrendered all and have died to everything we ever hoped, desired, or dreamed; allowed all roots of sin nature to be severed, cut off, pulled up from their roots; and have offered *our* final sacrifice, then we are now prepared to receive all of Him.

- His divine *power*
- His divine *authority*
- His divine *purpose*

to *change* even the very atmosphere around us.

Oh, the indescribable joy that we have prevailed and are now an overcomer! Now He fills us with all of Himself. Now He anoints all of Himself in us. Now we are His vessel through whom He now lives *His* life. Now everything we touch lives—His Life (not ours) flowing through us to others. It's glorious to be on this side of surrender. But if Jesus Himself had to surrender His human will and go through the Cross, how much more must we? There are no shortcuts! If we want all of Him, all our old Adamic nature must go. Now He directs our very steps. We go wherever He wants to go. We do whatever He wants to do. We live wherever He wants to live. Jesus is the precious, priceless Pearl!

There is no other!

He alone is God.

He loves us so!

Incredible joy is in your future—His joy!

PART VII: THE GLORY OF HIS PRESENCE

Step 18

Ribbons of Rejoicing

The thread of joy is like a shimmering gold ribbon.
Joy now floods us, and we feel alive with life! Life pulsates through us like a steady heartbeat. Like a small
boy flying his kite, we feel as if we are soaring higher
and higher into the heavens. And if we soar any higher
we will soon soar on the wings of angels. The old Adamic
nature is gone. The confrontation of the Cross is now
complete. The transformation is a reality. Joy inexpressible and full of glory has taken over.

Joy like a shimmering shadow of silk that infuses
every facet of our being. We know who we are and why
we are here. We know what our destiny is and our purpose in life. All this understanding brings great peace.

We have a new heart that has never known grief,
sadness, sorrow—only joy. This is the heart of David the
worshipper, the King of Israel following only after the
Lord. This is the heart of compassion. This is the heart
of the Lord. This is a heart that forgives and that loves.
This is a heart of *wholeness*, a heart with *passion* for

112

life. Simple joys—a sunset, a double rainbow, a baby's laugh, a sweet smile, whitecaps on the ocean, jumping in the sand, swimming, swinging, balancing one foot in front of the other on the curb where there are no side-walks—are full of childlike innocence such as it was in the Garden of Eden. The Tree of Life's roots are now dug deep in us with happy times, courageous times, sweet times, and laughing times abounding. Effervescent life is seen everywhere. The sky, mountains, ocean, wind, people are overflowing with living, breathing life. Life is ever moving—forward, up, around, over, ever reaching higher. Life—deep, abiding, penetrating life feels exhilarating. Our energy seems endless, and our fears are finished *forever.*

Some of the beauties of life that we see and experience:

- Bouncing baby bundles—two together—tiny, tender tots on tip toe.
- Silver ribbons rejoicing—bell-like clear, colorful, complete.
- Talks—happy, serene, silent, solo, distant.
- Party—pleasing precious pink purple balloons, billowing, beckoning to the sky.

All this on the inside of joy.

It is time now to rejoice. "Rejoice in the Lord always. I will say it again: Rejoice" (Phil. 4:4). It is as if the word "joy" has tiny capsules on the inside of it. Inside those capsules are what was previously described. Tiny sacs like cocoons in every part of that word—when you prick each cocoon sac another aspect of joy bursts forth into life. Joy—never ending, always expanding deeper until we go so deep, we reach the source of joy—Jesus Himself!

One day as I was worshipping the Lord at home and thanking Him for what He had done in my new life, the sun was shining brilliantly through the window. All of a sudden the brilliance increased and I saw in my spirit-man a Bible, brand new with silver edging on the pages. It was not mine. Mine was old and tear-stained, and lipstick kisses and tears were all over *The Song of Solomon*. It was as if an unseen hand were holding this brand new, pristine, silver-edged Bible. The Bible was held on its side and a wind came and blew it open to each page from Genesis to Revelation and only *one* word was spoken each time a page was turned by this breeze: "Jesus." I got it! Jesus is on every page of the Bible from Genesis to Revelation because "In the Beginning was the Word and the Word was with God and the Word was God. He was with God in the beginning" (John 1:1 and 2). He is the Alpha, the Omega, the Beginning and the End. The pre-incarnate Christ—Jesus is the Word from Genesis to Revelation. And Jesus is present in the New Testament—the Word took on flesh and became man. When I got it and the entire Bible had been opened from Genesis to Revelation, the "open vision" (my physical eyes were wide open yet I saw with my spiritual eyes) left as quickly as it had appeared.

Jesus the man—compassionate, gentle, kind, tough,
   tall, and true.
Jesus the man—anointed, wise, understanding, His
   love for us unconquerable.

Jesus the man—authority, commitment, blood
    poured out.
Jesus the man—was crushed on the Cross so the
    Cross would not crush you.
Jesus the man—suffered in hell for us.
And on the third day He rose triumphantly
    declaring, "You've been set free!"
The trumpets sounded
The heralds roared
Welcome the King
He has won
From eternity past
The present too
See a glimpse of what He has done for you.
His death was done, this deed to God's Son.
His special one lying in a grave though cold and dark
    could not keep this one so fair, and soon all
    would know He's no longer there!
For He has risen
Always to be
The Lord our King throughout eternity.
And so He has said
Grave, you can't keep Me
You must let go!
Now others will see
That my Father's Word is true through all eternity.
So come third day
Christians come to the Lamb
And let us celebrate
His victory over death, hell and the grave
As we partake of His Body, His precious Blood too
Which He poured out just for you.

As we take communion, we celebrate this life given so we may die to self and rise again a new creation encapsulated by His Life, Himself. He loves you so much more than you could ever know, so come let Him see you want to eat of the Tree of Life,
His knowledge,
His love,
His kindness,
His joy,
His sweetness,
His truth.

The trumpets sounded
The heralds roared
Welcome the King
He has scored
Victoriously over
Sickness and death
To bring to His Church
Complete wholeness
So come today
Come one and all
Can't you hear
His precious call?
The call of our King to His people below
Come up higher
And you will know
I've called you to sit in heavenly places
For you are kings and priests too
Come and I'll show
You what I did

Just for you
Enter My presence
And there you will find
Your Saviour, Your Lord
He is so kind
He loves you with love
Passion too
He loves you so much
He died just for you.
So come My Bride
I wait for you!

PRAYER OF SALVATION

Sweet friend, if you do not know Jesus, this wonderful, wonderful Jesus who died just for you, and you would like to know Him as your very own Lord and Saviour, would you please pray the following prayer?

Dear Heavenly Father,

I would like Jesus to come into my heart and be my Lord and Saviour. Your Word says in Romans 10:9-10 that if I confess out loud "Jesus is (my) Lord and believe in my heart God raised Him from the dead, I shall be saved. For it is with my heart that I believe and am *justified* (just as if I never sinned), and it is with my mouth that I confess and I am saved."

I now say the following, "Please Lord Jesus, come into my heart. Please be my Lord and my Saviour. I repent for the wrong life I have lived until now. I choose You and will live for You all the days of my life. Thank You, Lord Jesus. I love You. In Jesus' name, Amen."

You are now His child! All heaven is jumping up and down and dancing because you received Jesus into your very own heart. Tell someone you just received Jesus and find a great Christian Church and grow in Him. He loves you and desires worship from your heart each and every day. You are precious to Him.

Glory!

Come away,
my lover,
and be like a gazelle
or like a young stag
on the spice-laden
mountains."

(Song of Solomon 8:14)

About the Author

Reverend Helen Brock, who has lived in Hawaii for many years, came to America via Canada. Her late husband, Dr. Joseph A. Brock, who had an Ob-Gyn practice in Honolulu for more than 20 years, was formerly from California. Together they raised their children (some of whom were born in the Islands) in this beautiful paradise. Their four children, who are now young adults, are very talented and gifted. Their older son is a songwriter, record producer, and web designer; their older daughter is a future author of children's books; their younger daughter is an opera singer (a vocalist on Yanni's latest recording); and their younger son is a corporate/commercial pilot. They all presently live on the mainland. Two of them are married and have their own precious, gifted spouses and young family.

Since 1975, the year Helen and her husband became born-again, the author has been in ministry. This calling of God on her life has taken her most recently (1995) from Hawaii to the U.S. mainland, Europe, and Canada. Upon completion of this assignment (2002), seven years and a lifetime later, our Lord brought her full circle home to Hawaii. Now in the eighth year (the year of new beginnings), the birth of this book, *The Lover's Dance,* which was conceived in her in Honolulu, Hawaii, in 1991 has now become reality.

All glory, all honor be unto our God, our precious Lord Jesus Christ.

Hallelujah! For our Lord God Almighty reigns. Let us rejoice and be glad and give him glory! For the wedding of the Lamb has come, and his bride has made herself ready (Rev. 6b & 7).

To contact the author
for her speaking itinerary only, please write to:

Reverend Helen Leona Brock, Evangelist
Song of Solomon
"Three-part" New Creation
Bride of Christ Ministries, LLC
P.O. Box 10098
Honolulu, Hawaii 96816

Visit her website at: www.theloversdance.com